PREVENT
TEACH
REINFORCE

PREVENT
TEACH
REINFORCE

THE SCHOOL-BASED MODEL OF
INDIVIDUALIZED
POSITIVE BEHAVIOR SUPPORT

by

Glen Dunlap, Rose Iovannone, Donald Kincaid,

Kelly Wilson, Kathy Christiansen,

Phillip Strain, and Carie English

Baltimore • London • Sydney

Paul H. Brookes Publishing Co.
Post Office Box 10624
Baltimore, Maryland 21285-0624
USA

www.brookespublishing.com

Typeset by Spearhead Global, Inc., Bear, Delaware.
Manufactured in the United States of America by
Versa Press, Inc., East Peoria, Illinois.

The individuals described in this book are composites or real people whose situations are masked and are based on the authors' experiences. In all instances, names and identifying details have been changed to protect confidentiality.

Library of Congress Cataloging-in-Publication Data

Prevent-teach-reinforce : the school-based model of individualized positive behavior support / by Glen Dunlap ... [et al.].
   p.   cm.
   Includes bibliographical references and index.
   ISBN-13: 978-1-59857-015-1 (pbk. with cd)
   ISBN-10: 1-59857-015-3
   1. Behavioral assessment of children.   2. Problem children—Behavior modification.   3. School psychology.   I. Dunlap, Glen.   II. Title.
   LB1124.P74   2010
   371.102′4–dc22   2009036351

British Library Cataloguing in Publication data are available from the British Library.

2019   2018   2017   2016   2015
10   9   8   7   6   5   4

Contents

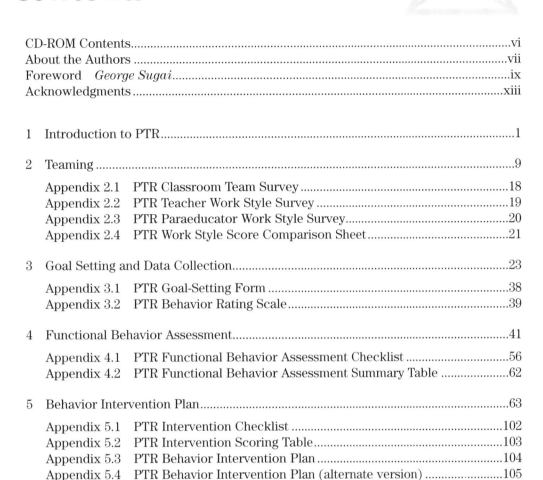

CD-ROM Contents

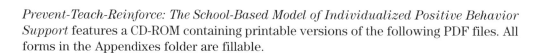

Prevent-Teach-Reinforce: The School-Based Model of Individualized Positive Behavior Support features a CD-ROM containing printable versions of the following PDF files. All forms in the Appendixes folder are fillable.

Appendix 2.1 PTR Classroom Team Survey
Appendix 2.2 PTR Teacher Work Style Survey
Appendix 2.3 PTR Paraeducator Work Style Survey
Appendix 2.4 PTR Work Style Score Comparison Sheet
Appendix 3.1 PTR Goal-Setting Form
Appendix 3.2 PTR Behavior Rating Scale
Appendix 4.1 PTR Functional Behavior Assessment Checklist
Appendix 4.2 PTR Functional Behavior Assessment Summary Table
Appendix 5.1 PTR Intervention Checklist
Appendix 5.2 PTR Intervention Scoring Table
Appendix 5.3 PTR Behavior Intervention Plan
Appendix 5.4 PTR Behavior Intervention Plan (alternate version)
Appendix 5.5 PTR Training Checklist
Appendix 5.6 PTR Fidelity of Implementation
Appendix 6.1 PTR Self-Evaluation: Social Validity

About the Authors

Glen Dunlap, Ph.D., Research Professor, Division of Applied Research and Educational Support (DARES), Department of Child & Family Studies, Florida Mental Health Institute, University of South Florida, Tampa, Florida 33612-3899

Dr. Dunlap is a research professor at the University of South Florida, where he works on several research, training, and demonstration projects in the areas of positive behavior support, child protection, early intervention, developmental disabilities, and family support. He has been involved with individuals with disabilities for more than 35 years and has served as a teacher, administrator, researcher, and university faculty member. Dr. Dunlap has directed numerous research and training projects and has been awarded dozens of federal and state grants to pursue this work. He has authored more than 185 articles and book chapters, coedited four books, and served on 15 editorial boards. Dr. Dunlap was a founding editor of the *Journal of Positive Behavior Interventions* and is the current editor of *Topics in Early Childhood Special Education.* He moved to Reno, Nevada, in 2005, where he continues to work on research and training projects as a member of the faculty at the University of South Florida.

Rose Iovannone, Ph.D., Assistant Professor, Division of Applied Research and Educational Support (DARES), Department of Child & Family Studies, Florida Mental Health Institute, University of South Florida, 13301 Bruce B. Downs Boulevard, MHC 2113A, Tampa, Florida 33612-3899

Dr. Iovannone is currently the director of the Prevent-Teach-Reinforce (PTR) Project. She has also served as the co-principal investigator on a University of South Florida (USF) subcontract for the Professional Development in Autism Project funded by Office of Special Education Programs (OSEP) and Assistant Director for the Center for Autism and Related Disabilities (CARD) at USF. She has published several journal articles and book chapters in the areas of functional assessment, function-based support plans, and positive behavior support and is currently working on numerous manuscripts related to preliminary outcomes of the PTR project. She teaches graduate-level courses on behavioral interventions. As an expert in providing support at the tertiary level, Dr. Iovannone is also a well-respected trainer and consultant. She has extensive experience in working with individuals with autism, learning disabilities, and emotional disabilities. Her principal activities and research interests have been in the areas of functional behavior assessment and positive behavior support, augmentative and alternative communication, and assessment and evaluation.

Donald Kincaid, Ed.D., Assistant Program Director and Professor, Division of Applied Research and Educational Support (DARES), Department of Child & Family Studies, Florida Mental Health Institute, University of South Florida, 13301 Bruce B. Downs Boulevard, MHC 2113A, Tampa, Florida 33612-3899

Dr. Kincaid is the director of the Florida Positive Behavior Support Project and the Principal Investigator of the Prevent-Teach-Reinforce model. He is also a collaborator and principal investigator for the University of South Florida's subcontract with the Technical Assistance Center for Positive Behavioral Interventions and Supports. He also serves as the co-principal investigator on Florida's Center for Inclusive Communities, a University Center for Excellence in Developmental Disabilities. His primary interests are in applying positive behavior support approaches for individual students, classrooms, and entire schools. Much of his professional activity involves coordinating systems change efforts at a local, state, and national level to support the implementation of evidence-based practices. Dr. Kincaid also teaches at the university level and serves on a number of editorial and advisory boards in the area of positive behavior support.

Kelly Wilson, Professional Research Assistant, Center for Positive Early Learning Experiences, Center for Collaborative Educational Leadership, School of Education and Human Development, University of Colorado at Denver, 1380 Lawrence Street, Suite 600, Denver, Colorado 80204

Ms. Wilson is a research assistant/consultant for the Center for Positive Early Learning Experiences at the University of Colorado at Denver. She is currently working on the PTR (Prevent-Teach-Reinforce) grant and the Learning Experiences: An Alternative Program for Preschoolers and Parents (LEAP) Outreach Project, providing consultation and training to elementary schools and preschools serving children with autism and challenging behaviors. Over the last 13 years, Ms. Wilson has been involved in almost every aspect of early intervention, general education, and special education. She has extensive experience as a trainer for children with special needs and challenging behavior in inclusive settings.

Kathy Christiansen, M.S., Assistant in Technical Assistance, Division of Applied Research and Educational Support (DARES), Department of Child & Family Studies, Florida Mental Health Institute, University of South Florida, 13301 Bruce B. Downs Boulevard, MHC 2113A, Tampa, Florida 33612-3899

Ms. Christiansen is a research assistant of Child and Family Studies at the University of South Florida (USF). She is currently a consultant with the Prevent-Teach-Reinforce Project and the Florida Positive Behavior Support Project. She also worked as a consultant with the Center for Autism and Related Disabilities (CARD) at USF. Before coming to USF, Ms. Christiansen worked as a district-level behavior specialist, special education teacher, and manager in residential programs for children and youth and was a therapeutic foster care provider for more than 5 years. She specializes in training and consultation for children with severe behavior problems.

Phillip Strain, Ph.D., Professor, School of Education and Human Development, University of Colorado at Denver, 1380 Lawrence Street, Suite 650, Denver, Colorado 80204-2076

Dr. Strain is a professor of Educational Psychology and Psychiatry at the University of Colorado at Denver. He is the author of more than 250 scientific papers and he serves on the editorial boards of more than a dozen professional journals. Dr. Strain has worked in the field of early intervention since 1974, and he serves as a science advisor to the Institute of Medicine, the National Institute of Mental Health, and the U.S. Department of Education. His primary research interests include intervention for young children with early-onset conduct disorders; remediation of social behavior deficits in young children with autism; design and delivery of community-based, comprehensive early intervention for children with autism; and analysis of individual and systemic variables affecting the adoption and sustained use of evidence-based practices for children with severe behavior disorders.

Carie English, Ph.D., 3315 West Pearl Avenue, Tampa, Florida 33611

Dr. English consults with and provides training to individuals and schools to develop and implement function-based interventions at all tiers of the behavioral triangle. As a research assistant professor of Child & Family Studies at the University of South Florida, she served as a behavior consultant with the Prevent-Teach-Reinforce Project and with the Florida Positive Behavior Support Project. Dr. English specializes in training and consultation with students with severe problem behavior. She has published in the area of functional assessment, functionally derived interventions, and positive behavior support and has taught courses at the university level on behavioral interventions.

Foreword

When I began my special education teaching career in Colorado in the 1970s, I thought I was well-equipped to educate students who were identified as seriously emotionally disturbed (SED). Under a brand new piece of legislation called the Education for All Handicapped Children Act of 1975 (PL 94-142), I was asked to set up one of the first middle school resource rooms. I ordered a stop-watch, a yellow pad of graph paper, and a clipboard to count the number of times a problem behavior occurred. I carefully summarized student scores from a battery of norm-referenced tests and took detailed notes when I interviewed teachers and parents about what they knew about the student. A team of us used this information to figure out if the student really needed the SED label and special education services. If the answer was "no," students were returned to the general education program to fend for themselves. If the SED label was deemed appropriate, we wrote an individualized education plan that described current level of functioning, short- and long-term objectives, specialized educational interventions, and percentage of the school day to be spent in my resource room.

In 1974, I considered my resource room to be state of the art. I had a programwide token economy and level system which was fully equipped with a classroom "store" filled with immediate and delayed middle school-appropriate back-up reinforcers and privileges, response–cost and time-out procedures for handling rule violations, and data-decision rules for movement up and down the levels. Each day, we conducted individual student meetings to go over points, provide "behavioral counseling," and determine whether we needed to "tweak" the interventions. We also had a whole-group social skills program, individualized behavioral contracts, standard behavior charts to record and monitor student progress, and individual work folders that were filled with worksheets from the general education curriculum. Needless to say, I thought my resource room was the "perfect" place for students who didn't fit in any other classroom, and I worked, for all practical purposes, in isolation from the general education program. From my perspective, these students needed behavioral interventions they could only get from me and my special place at the end of the hallway.

If we fast-forward to 2009, what we did in the 1970s looks relatively simplistic and incomplete. When I look back at my first teaching experiences, I frequently find myself wondering, "How much more effective could I have been if I had only known then what I know now?" Over the last 40 years, significant advances have been made by behavioral psychologists, special educators, and school psychologists. In 2009, behavioral support for students has expanded to all students, not just those with SED, and a comprehensive and positive systems approach has evolved with the following qualities:

1. Prevention is emphasized to decrease the likelihood of the development, occurrence, and intensification of problem behaviors.

2. Early screening and assessment are conducted regularly to identify students whose behaviors cause them to be at high risk for school failure.

3. A function-based approach is used for behavioral assessments and behavior support planning.

4. Antecedent-based strategies are considered to be at least as important, if not more so, than consequence-based interventions.

5. Supervision of student behavior is formalized, active, direct, and continuous.

6. Effective, efficient, and relevant social behaviors are taught (social skills instruction) to compete with occurrences of problem behavior and are linked to classroom- and schoolwide social behavior expectations.

7. Immediate environmental triggers and maintenance of consequences are considered in behavioral assessment and intervention planning.

8. The function of problem behavior, or maintaining outcomes of problem behavior, is used to improve how we select and teach acceptable alternative replacement behaviors.

9. The effectiveness of the larger teaching and learning context (i.e., schoolwide and classroomwide) is considered when conducting individual functional behavioral assessments and developing and implementing behavior intervention plans.

10. Students, peers, and members of the school, family, and community are included in supporting the educational programs of individual students.

11. The use of evidence-based academic *and* behavior practices and systems is emphasized.

12. Actively monitoring and evaluating implementation accuracy and consistency (fidelity/integrity) are important prerequisites to being able to examine student progress and responsiveness to intervention.

13. Supports for students with the most significant problem behaviors and mental health needs are presented within a wraparound process that is inclusive, ecological, person centered, and systems based.

14. Objective data-based decision making and monitoring of student progress and responsiveness to our interventions are used to ensure that our outcomes are socially important and relevant.

The main message is that our knowledge base for comprehensive behavior support has advanced in many significant ways since my initial teaching years. Clearly, behavior support for all students is much more preventive, inclusive, relevant, schoolwide, and accountable. The real question is "How does one incorporate this vast knowledge base into real school environments so implementers are accurate, fluent, and sustained in their implementation and student outcomes are maximized?"

In this manual, the authors have developed the Prevent-Teach-Reinforce (PTR) model as a perfect example of how the implementation of best practice can be organized to maximize effectiveness, "do-ability," and relevance. PTR is best described in the authors' own words as

> a standardized approach to the development and implementation of individualized, school-based positive behavior support….The PTR model was created in response to the critical need for a standardized and manualized approach that is effective and feasible in addressing serious behavior problems in typical school circumstances.

Many "packaged" approaches lack a conceptually sound foundation from which to explain the mechanism by which practices work and for how results are achieved. PTR is grounded in strong and defendable theory—specifically, applied behavior analysis and positive behavior support. In addition, the authors have conducted the empirical and evaluation research that specifically documents the functional relationship between PTR as the main independent variable and improvements in behavioral outcomes as the dependent variables (Dunlap, Iovannone, Wilson, Kincaid, & Strain, in press; Iovannone et al., in press). This research, in general, documents that students who have received manualized PTR interventions, in contrast to usual intervention services, had improved social skills and academic engagement, reduced rates of problem behaviors, and high acceptance by implementing teachers.

The importance of a workable behavioral curriculum cannot be stressed enough. The authors and developers of PTR have made the model accessible to real school implementers by creating efficient forms that prompt and instruct the user on how they are to be completed. The manual has a full range of examples that illustrate each step and substep of the PTR process. To ensure quality implementation, practical "suggestions," implementation considerations, and self-assessment checklists are provided. Evaluation practices and guidelines enable users to conduct continuous progress monitoring that informs current implementation fidelity and future programmatic enhancements. Finally, an excellent sample of references is included to enhance user confidence about intervention efficacy and to enable more in-depth study.

The real attraction of the PTR approach is the immediately accessible three-principle logic of PTR. Redesigning teaching and learning environments to maximize teaching and learning is given priority over traditional consequence-only behavior reduction strategies. First, *Prevent* emphasizes how critical it is to engage in practices early and frequently by

1. Redesigning teaching and learning environments to inhibit the development of problem behavior patterns

2. Selecting acceptable alternative behaviors that work equally as well or better than problem behaviors

3. Removing antecedent stimuli that trigger and consequence stimuli that maintain occurrences of problem behavior

4. Adding antecedent stimuli that trigger and consequence stimuli that increase occurrences of appropriate behavior

Teach highlights the importance of directly and explicitly arranging opportunities to teach appropriate social behaviors. The authors approach teaching social behavior like teaching academic skills. Whether one is teaching a learner how to "calculate the hypotenuse of a right-angle triangle," "respond to teasing," "spell *responsibility*," "request assistance," "identify the main idea of a paragraph," or "settle a disagreement with an adult," the instructional steps are fundamentally the same:

1. Define and describe "it."

2. Give a range of positive and negatives examples for "it."

3. Model "it."

4. Arrange opportunities for learner to practice "it" in controlled contexts or settings with guidance and immediate feedback.

5. Arrange opportunities for learner to practice "it" in natural contexts or settings without assistance and with delayed feedback.

6. Reinforce all approximations of "it."

The *Reinforce* step is equally as important as Prevent and Teach. Shaping high-quality learner responses that are durable and generalizable requires systematic planning for contingent and positively reinforcing feedback. The authors present excellent guidelines for correcting errors, shaping approximations of desired responses, adjusting schedules of reinforcement to move learners through the phases of learning (i.e., acquisition, fluency, maintenance, generalized responding), and shifting from other- to self-manipulated reinforcement.

To summarize, the PTR approach and manual are based on sound behavioral theory, guided by a solid conceptual logic, operationalized by a solid set of empirically sound behavioral practices, organized in a highly doable and implementable format, and supported by an excellent set of efficient and generalizable forms and tools. My only "complaint" is that Glen Dunlap and his coauthors didn't have their PTR manual done in the '70s when I really could have used it to be a better teacher!

George Sugai, Ph.D.
University of Connecticut

REFERENCES

Dunlap, G., Iovannone, R., Wilson, K.J., Kincaid, D.K., & Strain, P. (in press). Prevent-Teach-Reinforce: A standardized model of school-based behavioral intervention. *Journal of Positive Behavior Interventions*.

Iovannone, R., Greenbaum, P.E., Wang, W., Kincaid, D., Dunlap, G., & Strain, P. (in press). Randomized controlled trial of the Prevent-Teach-Reinforce (PTR) tertiary intervention for students with problem behaviors: Preliminary outcomes. *Journal of Emotional and Behavioral Disorders*.

Acknowledgments

This book had its origins as a field manual that described the Prevent-Teach-Reinforce (PTR) model and guided participating teachers and school teams in the model's application. These teachers and team members were from several school districts in Florida (Hillsborough County Public Schools, Pasco County Schools and Pinellas County Schools) and Colorado (Denver Public Schools and Mesa County Valley School District 51). They were participants in an experimental evaluation of the PTR approach. We are grateful for their efforts and for the feedback they provided, and we appreciate the school districts for allowing and facilitating the implementation of PTR. Similarly, we acknowledge and extend our thanks to the students and their families who participated in the research.

The research conducted on the PTR model was funded by the Institute for Education Science (IES; Grant H324P04003); however, the contents of this book do not necessarily represent the policy of IES or the U.S. Department of Education, and no endorsement by the Federal Government should be assumed.

We wish to thank Rebecca Lazo and several other competent and encouraging staff of Paul H. Brookes Publishing Co. who were extremely supportive throughout the process of producing the book. Rebecca was (and is) a true friend in addition to being a skilled editor and facilitator.

PREVENT
TEACH
REINFORCE

Introduction

This book is intended to describe the Prevent-Teach-Reinforce (PTR) model of behavioral support and to guide school-based teams through the PTR process. PTR is a systematic, structured process for supporting students with challenging behavior. In particular, PTR is an approach for students with challenging behaviors that have not been resolved satisfactorily with classroom and schoolwide behavior management systems. This model is an option for students with persistent challenging behaviors that have created significant barriers to instruction for the student and classmates.

PTR is based on extensive research with a wide variety of students and is intended for all students with challenging behavior, including students with disabilities (Dunlap, Iovannone, Wilson, Kincaid, & Strain, in press). PTR is a model of positive behavior support (PBS) and is aligned largely with the principles and procedures of applied behavior analysis (ABA). Among the ABA principles used by PTR are functional behavior assessment (FBA) procedures, reinforcement of desired alternative behaviors, shaping of new behaviors, fading of prompts and reinforcement, and contingency management approaches.

PTR can be used with students at all levels of functioning and is designed for students in kindergarten to eighth grade. It can be used with students in general education classrooms, as well as students with learning disabilities, intellectual disabilities, emotional and behavior disorders, autism, and other challenges of development, learning, and behavior. However, PTR may be of limited effectiveness if the challenging behaviors are related to or caused by medical or physiological factors or temporary disruptions in a student's living situation. If medical factors, physiological factors, or severe disruptions in the student's home life are suspected, it is recommended that appropriate professionals address these factors before initiating the PTR process.

There are five steps in the PTR process: teaming, goal setting, assessment, intervention, and evaluation. These steps are described in detail in Chapters 2–6. The process for completing the steps is the same for all students. In this way, the PTR model is a standardized approach. However, the content that is developed within each step is based on the student's characteristics, as well as the characteristics of the setting and the school professionals who will be responsible for implementing the intervention. Thus, the model is both standardized to meet the needs of all students, yet individualized to address the special characteristics and circumstances of the student in need of assistance.

The PTR intervention phase consists of at least three components. Interventions for all participating students include procedures involving prevention, teaching, and reinforcement. In the Prevent component, changes are made in the student's activities, settings, or social circumstances. The Teach component involves selecting and teaching new skills that will give the student an alternative to the challenging behavior. In the Reinforce component, effective and appropriate motivators are selected and used to encourage desirable, prosocial behavior. The specific strategies to be used for each of the components are selected by the school-based team using PTR assessments, along with careful consideration of what will be feasible to implement. One of the requirements for effective use of the PTR model is that students receive at least some intervention support from each of the three components.

POSITIVE BEHAVIOR SUPPORT AND APPLIED BEHAVIOR ANALYSIS

PTR is derived from two powerful approaches that have guided behavior support for several decades. The first is PBS, which is a broad approach for organizing environmental, social, educational, and systems strategies to improve the competence and quality of life for individuals with problems of behavioral adaptation. PBS seeks to reduce the occurrence of challenging behavior because such problems interfere with development, learning, and positive relationships with adults and peers. PBS is a positive approach in that it avoids harsh and stigmatizing punishments and emphasizes instruction and environmental arrangements to achieve desired outcomes. PBS emerged as a useful approach in the mid-1980s from a number of foundations, including ABA (Bambara & Kern, 2005; Carr et al., 2002; Dunlap, 2006; Dunlap, Carr, Horner, Zarcone, & Schwartz, 2008).

ABA is a scientific discipline in which principles of learning are applied to produce socially meaningful changes in a person's behavior. It is a discipline that has been applied in a great number of fields, including education, social work, psychology, child development, and business. Research conducted over approximately 50 years has clearly demonstrated the validity and numerous contributions of ABA. It is important to understand that ABA can be manifested in many ways. Programs that are strongly rooted in ABA may appear to be very different when they are, in fact, based on the same conceptual and philosophical foundations (Cooper, Heron, & Heward, 2007).

Many educators may be confronted with questions about the distinctions between PTR, PBS, and ABA. The PTR model is directly linked to PBS, and it is also derived from the principles and procedures of ABA. In brief, PTR is a specific model that is part of PBS. PTR is entirely consistent with the PBS approach, although PBS can be implemented in various ways and at various levels of application. PBS also is derived from the foundations of ABA. Although PBS is different enough to warrant its own label, it also is similar enough to ABA that some practitioners of ABA use strategies that are indistinguishable from PBS (Dunlap et al., 2008). ABA broadly refers to a widespread discipline that can accommodate many practices and programs. The resources listed at the end of this chapter may be useful for readers who are interested in pursuing further the definitions and distinctions of PBS and ABA.

RESEARCH FOUNDATIONS OF PTR

The PTR model is based on extensive research on the components of PBS, the PBS process as a whole, and findings from a large-scale experimental evaluation of PTR in schools in multiple locations in Florida and Colorado (Iovannone et al., in press). The process and procedures that make up the components of PTR have been studied and refined for decades under the auspices of PBS and ABA. For example, in support of the PTR assessment process, there are a plethora of experimental studies that have verified the validity of FBA and the benefits that accrue from preceding intervention with functional assessment strategies (e.g., Repp & Horner, 1999; Umbreit, Ferro, Liaupsin, & Lane, 2007). A similarly large number of studies have documented the effectiveness of environmental and antecedent manipulations (the Prevent component of the PTR model; e.g., Luiselli, 2006), as well as instructional and reinforcement approaches (the Teach and Reinforce components; e.g., Bambara & Kern, 2005; Halle, Bambara, & Reichle, 2005). A number of research syntheses and reviews have examined the components and the entire process of PBS and found them to be effective with many populations of children with challenging behaviors (e.g., Bambara & Kern, 2005; Carr et al., 1999; Dunlap & Carr, 2007; Sailor, Dunlap, Sugai, & Horner, 2009).

A direct, experimental examination of the efficacy of the PTR process was conducted in several school districts in Florida and Colorado. In this investigation, children with the most severe challenging behaviors were randomly assigned into either the PTR group or a comparison group that was provided with the districts' usual approach. Preliminary analyses of data from 205 students revealed significant beneficial effects of PTR on reducing the occurrence of challenging behavior, increasing evidence of social skills, and increasing the occurrence of academic engaged time (Iovannone et al., in press).

THE FIVE-STEP PROCESS OF PTR

The PTR process presented in this book is similar to the PBS sequence described elsewhere. However, we have made efforts to create a progression that is specific in its details and as easy to follow as possible. Furthermore, we have tested the model with a diversity of students in dozens of classrooms in school districts in Florida and Colorado. In all cases, the school's professional staff—especially the teachers—have been the key designers and implementers of the individualized PTR interventions. For this reason, we are confident that the model will be effective with the majority of students, regardless of how challenging and persistent a student's behavior has been.

The PTR model consists of five steps. The remaining chapters each represent one of the steps. Each step is accompanied by objectives and a recommended pathway for meeting the objectives. To ensure success, the objectives associated with each chapter should be completed before moving to the next chapter. The following sections provide a brief introduction of each step.

Team Building

The first step in the PTR process is the establishment of a well-functioning team consisting of individuals who are responsible for the intervention and invested in the well-being of the student. Although a team approach is not always necessary for delivering effective behavior support, it is necessary if the student's challenging behaviors are serious, chronic, and/or intensive. Because PTR is intended for this group of students, the team approach is an essential element of the process. A team usually includes three to seven individuals; it must include the student's teacher and any other school employee who spends substantial time with the student. The team must also include an individual who is knowledgeable about behavioral approaches and experienced with FBA, assessment-based interventions, and PBS. In addition, it is desirable to have team members who are parents or other primary caregivers, administrators or school professionals with direct access to school resources and policies, and anyone else who cares about the student and is in a position to facilitate optimal interventions.

Goal Setting and Data Collection

Once a team has been established, the second step is to develop a clear consensus regarding the short- and long-term goals for the student. This unity of vision is critical to ensure that all team members are working in the same direction and share an understanding about the real priorities that are to guide the intervention plan. Often these goals have already been developed in the form of an individualized education program, but it is nevertheless important for the team to review such goals and determine if they are the most significant for this phase of the student's development. When goals are agreed upon, practical data collection strategies are developed to evaluate the status of the student's behavior, evaluate progress, and determine whether revisions to the intervention plan are needed. Data collection procedures should be simple for typical classroom personnel to implement.

PTR Assessment

The third step in the process is a version of an FBA. The PTR Assessment is structured so that all team members contribute information that relates to the three key components of the intervention: Prevent, Teach, and Reinforce. The assessment process involves answering a series of questions that are then summarized to represent a functional understanding of the student's challenging behaviors and how they are influenced by events in the social, instructional, and physical environment.

PTR Intervention

The fourth step involves using the results of the PTR Assessment to create an individualized intervention plan. Menus are provided to help teams select intervention strategies that are apt to be effective and fit well within the school settings where they will be used. At least one strategy is selected from menus in each of the three components of Prevent, Teach, and Reinforce.

Evaluation

The final step in the process is evaluation. Chapter 6 describes realistic procedures for evaluating the effects of the PTR intervention and indicates what teachers and team members can do on the basis of evaluation results.

EFFECTIVE IMPLEMENTATION OF PTR

The PTR model was tested over several years in dozens of classrooms. It is clear that the model can lead to meaningful improvements in students' behavior and academic achievement. Some factors are associated with the most desirable outcomes, whereas other factors may militate against improvement. The factors that contribute to the effectiveness of the PTR model include the following.

1. **A commitment to successful outcomes for students**

   The commitment to successful outcomes for students is critical at the district, school administrator, and student team levels. At the district level, the district has to develop and strongly endorse an FBA and behavior intervention plan process that is designed to prevent serious challenging behavior and support students to remain in typical educational settings. Implementation of a process like PTR will likely be insufficient if the philosophy of the district includes an explicit or implicit position that an FBA and behavior intervention plan are to be implemented for the primary purpose of meeting the legal requirements for removing a student from a neighborhood school or least restrictive environment.

   A philosophy of commitment to supporting students in their current educational settings must also be mirrored at the school by administrators and the school team. Many of the changes identified in the PTR process require changes at the school, classroom, and teacher levels. Without building administrators who are willing to commit time and resources to the PTR process, the PTR plan is unlikely to be implemented with fidelity. Fidelity of implementation, in this case, refers to whether all of the PTR components are implemented completely, accurately, and as often as necessary to produce desired outcomes for students. In addition, the more committed team members are to "making it work," the more likely it is that the PTR intervention model will be effective.

2. **Fidelity of implementation**

   The greater the extent to which the intervention team (e.g., teachers) is able to implement the plan as intended, the more effective it will be. Although the data do not indicate that an intervention has to be implemented with 100% fidelity to be effective (i.e., some interventions may still work if they are done with intermittent fidelity), it is likely that interventions that are implemented infrequently and inconsistently will not produce the intended outcomes for students. If the team is implementing with very high fidelity and the plan is still not as effective as anticipated, it is time to reevaluate the plan and consider revisions to the intervention strategies.

3. **Capacity of the team members**

   As indicated previously, it is important to have a team member (or consultant to the team) who is familiar with behavioral theory and experienced with the core elements of the PTR process, especially FBA and assessment-based interventions. In addition, the team will benefit from the support of a consultant or team member with team leadership skills, which might include the ability to ask reflective questions, support participants in sharing their opinions, and build rapport with and between team members. Finally, the team will be most successful in addressing very difficult behavioral or implementation situations if they approach issues within a problem-solving paradigm. A typical problem-solving process may include identifying the problem, understanding the problem, developing strategies to address the problem, and evaluating the effectiveness of the strategies. During the PTR process, there will be many opportunities for a team to practice a problem-solving process to overcome hurdles that may have an impact on the success of the PTR process.

4. **Availability, involvement, and support of school administrators**

   To address the behavioral needs of the most challenging students, it is often necessary to have access to special resources, permission to attend meetings, and occasional flexibility with respect to school policies. In addition, the team members need to know that their efforts are encouraged and supported by supervisors and other school officials. As mentioned previously, commitment to and direct involvement in the team's activities by pertinent school administrators is a key factor in heightening the probability of favorable outcomes.

5. **Family involvement**

   If the team can incorporate the involvement of family members, the overall outcomes are likely to be better. Even though the focus of the PTR intervention may be on school behavior, parents and other family members may have useful tips and results of previous interventions to contribute. Furthermore, if the family is involved with the development and implementation of the school intervention, there is a chance that parts of the plan may be carried out at home, thereby promoting some generalization of the effects. If family members are unable to attend team meetings, they can still be informed of the discussions, decisions, and actions related to the PTR process.

LIMITATIONS AND ACCOMMODATIONS

The PTR approach will not be effective in every situation. First, there are some factors that may contribute to challenging behaviors that are beyond the capacity of PTR to address. For instance, some students experience neurological and/or medical conditions that are not amenable to the educational and behavioral intervention strategies of PTR. Uncontrolled seizures, chronic illness, or neurological syndromes (e.g., Tourette syndrome) can contribute to the presence of challenging behavior, but it would be inappropriate to attempt to resolve such problems with strictly educational-behavioral procedures. Under such circumstances, it is vital that appropriate medical, neurological, and psychiatric services are obtained.

Similarly, some students may experience major disruptions in their home environments. Such disruptions may result in problems with a student's emotional and behavioral functioning. The PTR approach is not designed to address serious problems that occur beyond the school setting. While PTR may be helpful for school behavior, it is clear that more services will be required in these circumstances before the full source of the problems can be resolved (e.g., Duchnowski & Kutash, 2009; Eber, Hyde, Rose, Breen, McDonald, & Lewandowski, 2009).

There will also be times when, despite the best efforts of the school-based team, the PTR approach does not produce fully adequate behavior change. For example, the child's behavior in question may be so serious (e.g., hurting animals, setting fires, injuring self or others), infrequent, or unobservable that it is impossible to complete an adequate school-based FBA. In this situation, staff may be at a loss to determine the function of the challenging behavior and therefore cannot implement an individualized intervention. For serious challenging behaviors that rarely occur or occur when adults may not typically be present, it may be necessary to obtain outside help to monitor the child on something close to an around-the-clock basis. Such monitoring should have the completion of a reliable FBA as its end point. In addition, programs may want to solicit a diagnostic evaluation by a licensed child psychologist or psychiatrist for behaviors that have a covert quality to them (i.e., the child seems to purposely engage in challenging behavior when adults are absent). The goal of this assistance should be to determine if other supports and/or professionals need to be involved in this child's life.

In other situations, the team may have designed an individualized intervention plan and implemented the plan with fidelity, but the child's behavior has not been altered over a period of several weeks. In this case, we first recommend repeating the FBA to confirm the communicative message of the challenging behavior. It is not uncommon for a behavior to be found originally to serve one function, and then subsequently found to serve different and/or multiple functions. Should this step not yield satisfactory results, it may be appropriate to call on a consultant who is more experienced in FBA. This individual may decide to use alternative observation procedures to analyze behavior, more thoroughly explore the possible role of setting events external to school, or ask staff to briefly try interventions that are consistent with several different functions. When using this type of consultative help, it is vital that staff become trained to implement the methods used by the consultant.

SUMMARY

PTR is a specific approach for school personnel to use when confronted with a student who demonstrates persistent and serious challenging behaviors. It is applicable for students from kindergarten through eighth grade and for students with a broad range of developmental and intellectual characteristics. There is an extensive base of research to document the effectiveness of PTR's components, as well as the model as a whole.

This book is intended to assist school personnel to proceed through the five steps of the PTR process. Chapters 2–6 will focus on one step and include objectives, tools, and recommendations. Each chapter also includes tips addressing considerations that deserve special emphasis or that identify essential aspects of the assessment and intervention process. The content of the chapters is designed to be specific enough for school personnel to follow the process without difficulty. If the steps are followed carefully and with precision, evidence indicates that there is a good likelihood that the student's behavior will improve in meaningful ways.

RESOURCES

Bambara, L., & Kern, L. (Eds.). (2005). *Individualized supports for students with problem behaviors: Designing positive behavior plans.* New York: Guilford Press.

Carr, E.G., Dunlap, G., Horner, R.H., Koegel, R.L., Turnbull, A.P., Sailor, W., et al. (2002). Positive behavior support: Evolution of an applied science. *Journal of Positive Behavior Interventions, 4,* 4–16.

Cooper, J.O., Heron, T.E., & Heward, W.L. (2007). *Applied behavior analysis.* Upper Saddle River, NJ: Pearson Merrill.

Duchnowski, A.J., & Kutash, K. (2009). Integrating PBS, mental health services, and family-driven care. In W. Sailor, G. Dunlap, G. Sugai, & R. Horner (Eds.), *Handbook of positive behavior support* (pp. 203–231). New York: Springer.

Dunlap, G. (2006). The applied behavior analytic heritage of PBS: A dynamic model of action-oriented research. *Journal of Positive Behavior Interventions, 8,* 58–60.

Dunlap, G., & Carr, E.G. (2007). Positive behavior support and developmental disabilities: A summary and analysis of research. In S.L. Odom, R.H. Horner, M. Snell, & J. Blacher (Eds.), *Handbook of developmental disabilities* (pp. 469–482). New York: Guilford.

Dunlap, G., Carr, E.G., Horner, R.H., Zarcone, J., & Schwartz, T.R. (2008). Positive behavior support and applied behavior analysis: A familial alliance. *Behavior Modification, 32,* 682–698.

Dunlap, G., Iovannone, R., Wilson, K., Kincaid, D., & Strain, P. (in press). Prevent-Teach-Reinforce: A standardized model of school-based behavioral intervention. *Journal of Positive Behavior Interventions.*

Eber, L., Hyde, K., Rose, J., Breen, K., McDonald, D., & Lewandowski, H. (2009). Completing the continuum of schoolwide positive behavior support: Wraparound as a tertiary-level intervention. In W. Sailor, G. Dunlap, G. Sugai, & R. Horner (Eds.), *Handbook of positive behavior support* (pp. 671–703). New York: Springer.

Halle, J., Bambara, L.M., & Reichle, J. (2005). Teaching alternative skills. In L. Bambara & L. Kern (Eds.), *Individualized supports for students with problem behaviors: Designing positive behavior plans* (pp. 237–274). New York: Guilford Press.

Iovannone, R., Greenbaum, P., Wei, W., Kincaid, D., Dunlap, G., & Strain, P. (in press). Randomized control trial of a tertiary behavior intervention for students with problem behaviors: Preliminary outcomes. *Journal of Emotional and Behavioral Disorders.*

Luiselli, J.K. (Ed.). (2006). *Antecedent assessment and intervention: Supporting children and adults with developmental disabilities in community settings.* Baltimore: Paul H. Brookes Publishing Co.

Repp, A.C., & Horner, R.H. (Eds.). (1999). *Functional analysis of problem behavior: From effective assessment to effective support.* Belmont, CA: Wadsworth Publishing Co.

Sailor, W., Dunlap, G., Sugai, G., & Horner, R.H. (Eds.). (2009). *Handbook of positive behavior support.* New York: Springer.

Umbreit, J., Ferro, J., Liaupsin, C., & Lane, K.L. (2007). *Functional behavioral assessment and function-based intervention: An effective, practical approach.* Englewood Cliffs, NJ: Pearson Merrill.

Teaming

OVERVIEW AND OBJECTIVES

The first step of the Prevent-Teach-Reinforce (PTR) model is to develop a cohesive, school-based team committed to helping students with significant challenging behaviors. The team should include individuals who have direct experience with the student and the behavior, as well as individuals who will be responsible for implementing the intervention. The size and composition of the team is determined by the needs of the student, the student's classroom teacher, and the school environment. Once the specific team members are identified, the group will determine their preferred approach to teaming and creating a collaborative, positive environment in which to meet.

Chapter 2 focuses on the following objectives:

- Developing a school-based team

- Determining an effective approach to teaming

- Identifying key elements for developing a collaborative teaming environment

- Outlining team roles and responsibilities

In achieving the objectives of this chapter, the following forms may be helpful: PTR Classroom Team Survey, Teacher Work Style Survey, Paraeducator Work Style Survey, and Work Style Score Comparison (see Appendixes 2.1–2.4, respectively; French, 2002). Blank copies of these forms are also included on the accompanying CD.

TIP

Team members should include the classroom teacher, others who will be responsible for implementing the intervention, and someone with knowledge about behavioral principles and positive behavior support.

TEAM MEMBERSHIP AND TEAM MEETINGS

When considering the composition of the school-based team, first identify those individuals who work closely with the student, have intimate knowledge of the student and the student's behaviors, and have a vested interest in assisting the student with positive behavior change. The student's primary classroom teacher must be a member of the team, whether the student is in a general or special education class. In addition, the student's parents or primary caregivers will be valuable members of the team. Other team members may include resource teachers, paraprofessionals, or related service providers such as occupational, physical, and speech therapists. It is especially important to include individuals on the team who interact with the student on a regular basis. Second, individuals who have knowledge of behavioral principles should be part of the student's team. This may be the school psychologist, social worker, behavior analyst, behavior specialist, special educator, or guidance counselor. Finally, an individual who has knowledge of the context and resources available should be included. This may be the school administrator or other designee who can interpret policy and provide access to resources. The number of members will vary from team to team based on the individual needs of the student. However, it is essential that at least one member of the team be knowledgeable regarding behavioral principles and positive behavior support, and have experience and training in the development and implementation of effective intervention strategies.

The actual number of meetings that are needed to complete the PTR process depends on the complexity of the student's challenging behaviors and the logistical details involved in developing a function-based intervention that is effective in achieving the established goals. For students with long-lasting challenging behavior that is resistant to change, a relatively large team and at least one meeting for each step in the PTR process may be necessary. When the behavior is fairly easy to understand and involves an intervention that is easy to design and implement, the team may only need a few members and one or two meetings. In either case, it is important that the team members interact in a collaborative and productive manner. Aspects of team functioning are discussed in the following sections.

TEAMING MODELS

The PTR model requires a team to share information, ask questions, address concerns, and engage in a collaborative process to develop an effective behavior intervention plan for the student with challenging behaviors. Each member comes to the team with his or her own beliefs about and experiences with various teams. Therefore, it is valuable for the PTR team to first determine their general philosophy about how the team will function, solve problems, and resolve conflicts. Whenever possible, incorporate the PTR process into already established teaming systems, such as RTI teams, keeping in mind the following teaming models.

Some teams use a multidisciplinary approach to the teaming process. A multidisciplinary team includes members from different disciplines or concentrations who complete activities independently, meet less frequently as a group, and usually communicate informally with one another. Within a multidisciplinary approach, each member meets individually with families, conducts assessments, prepares reports, and independently develops and implements interventions based upon his or her particular discipline. Some members of a multidisciplinary team may not even view themselves as part of a team. Related service providers (e.g., speech therapists, occupational therapists, physical therapists) often use this approach due to their multiple-site caseloads. One benefit to using a multidisciplinary approach to teaming is that members are able to pool their expertise to enhance the decision-making process. Combining resources and knowledge may reduce mistakes and biases. However, a multidisciplinary team may have difficulty creating a unified approach to interventions across disciplines. They may also be challenged by a lack of cohesion and commitment among team members.

Another form of teaming is the interdisciplinary approach, in which members share responsibility for services among disciplines. Interdisciplinary teams meet regularly for staffing and/or consultation. Families are encouraged to work in conjunction with the team. Within this approach, each team member conducts assessments and develops goals based on his or her discipline or area of concentration (i.e., the teacher assesses academic abilities, the behavior specialist completes the behavioral assessment). The results of the assessments then are formally shared with other members and a cohesive intervention plan is developed by the entire team. Once a behavior plan is created, each member of the team is responsible for implementing specific portions of the plan based on his or her discipline or area of expertise. Teams that use the interdisciplinary approach may find it easier to develop goals and plan activities that complement and support the other disciplines represented within the team. This enhances the team's commitment to a unified intervention plan. Within the interdisciplinary team, information flow is typically coordinated through a facilitator or case manager.

A third approach to the teaming process is the transdisciplinary method. This philosophy of teaming provides a framework in which team members commit to teach, learn, and work across job-specific boundaries in planning and providing integrated services. Transdisciplinary teams meet regularly to share information, participate in consultation, and enhance team cohesion. In this approach, job roles are often shared across members and disciplines. For example, a behavior specialist may take the lead in collecting behavioral data, while the classroom teacher may implement an academic intervention. Although each member maintains his or her area of expertise, roles and responsibilities are learned and shared. In a transdisciplinary approach to teaming, families are active members of the team and determine their own roles. The team often participates in arena-like assessments, which involve observing and recording across disciplines. This method allows multiple team members to view the same event and provide input. Together, the school staff and family members develop an intervention plan to address school and family concerns, resources, and priorities. Team members share responsibilities; everyone on the team is accountable for the plan's implementation, which ensures greater consistency and generalization.

TIP *Although adopting a transdisciplinary model is not a prerequisite to successful PTR implementation, this model is strongly recommended because of its association with consistency of programming across providers.*

The transdisciplinary approach to teaming has several benefits. First, it allows for more complete understanding of the student and provides a unified behavior intervention plan. It may also lead to professional growth by increasing the knowledge and skills of each team member. Although this approach requires the participation of many team members, it places the greatest responsibility on the teacher as the agent of change. Many teams may be challenged by transdisciplinary teaming because it requires a high degree of coordination and interaction between team members to ensure joint planning and meeting time. However, a behavior plan that has been developed collaboratively across disciplines will likely be more effective, be implemented with higher fidelity, and yield a greater impact on child outcomes.

The PTR Classroom Team Survey (see Appendix 2.1) will help the team to determine their strengths and weaknesses, as well as their current approach to the teaming process (French, 2002). This form may be completed individually by each team member or together as a group. It serves as a tool to enhance discussion. Once the form has been completed, the team may refer back to the teaming methods noted above to determine which approach most closely resembles the team's current process. The team should also discuss what changes may need to occur to achieve the desired approach to teaming. In addition to the PTR Classroom Team Survey, addressing the following questions may help the team to establish a preferred approach to the PTR teaming process:

- Is it important that every member attend every meeting (or most meetings)?

- Is every team member's input equally important?

- Does the team gather information from the student's family or is the family viewed as a member of the team?

- Do team members prefer to have informal meetings (i.e., disseminating information only) or formal meetings (i.e., sharing information, concerns, and/or ideas; gaining consensus on relevant issues)?

- Do members prefer to complete assessments and develop strategies for intervention separately by discipline or together as a team?

- Do individual members prefer to remain focused within their own concentrations or share responsibility for services across disciplines?

The PTR model is most effective when using the transdisciplinary approach to teaming. For the PTR process to be successful, the following elements need to be in place:

- All essential team members are identified.

- A specific team is established.

- A commitment to fully participate throughout the process is made by each team member.

- All team members agree to meet as scheduled.

- Every team member is a full and active contributor to the PTR process.

COLLABORATIVE TEAMING

Once the group members determine their preferred approach to teaming, they will address strategies for developing a cohesive team committed to helping the student. It is imperative for the team to develop a collaborative, nonthreatening environment in which to meet. Creating and maintaining a positive atmosphere contributes to the quality and effectiveness of communication and allows for the free exchange of ideas. Several characteristics of highly effective, collaborative teams have been identified (Appley & Winder, 1977; Larson, & LaFasto, 1989; Vandercook & York, 1990; Villa, Thousand, Paolucci-Whitcomb, & Nevin, 1990). Some of these characteristics include

- Establishing a climate of trust through honest and open communication

- Working to achieve a common, agreed-on goal

- Believing that all members have their own unique areas of expertise

- Placing significant value on every member's input

- Demonstrating mutual support for all the decisions that are made

- Agreeing on expectations and sharing responsibility for work that must done

Supervision and Work Styles

To create an effective collaborative team, it is useful for each member to examine his or her personal beliefs and practices with respect to working with others. Because team members have unique knowledge and abilities, it is valuable to identify each member's preferred communication, supervision, and work style. The PTR Teacher Work Style Survey and Paraeducator Work Style Survey (see Appendixes 2.2 and 2.3, respectively) will assist the teacher and paraprofessional(s) in this process (French, 2002). Sample questions from each form are provided in Figure 2.1.

After the teacher and paraeducator(s) have completed the forms individually, the team may choose to transfer the information to the PTR Work Style Score Comparison Sheet in Appendix 2.4 (French, 2002). When reviewing the PTR Work Style Score Comparison Sheet, the team should look for responses that are similar, which may indicate strengths or weaknesses between the teacher and paraeducator. The team should also look for contrasting responses, which may indicate ways to complement or balance the abilities and/or personal work styles of the teacher and paraeducator(s).

In the example in Figure 2.2, questions 1 and 17 have contrasting responses between the paraeducator and teacher. In question 1, the paraeducator indicates that he or she does not like to be closely supervised, whereas the teacher's response indicates a desire to supervise staff more closely. In question 17, the paraeducator prefers not to discuss activities with unfavorable results, but the teacher strongly agrees with the need to discuss problematic situations. It is important for the team to discuss the sharp contrast between the

PTR Teacher Work Style Survey—Sample

        Disagree Agree

1. I like to supervise the paraeducators closely...1 2 3 4 5 N/A
2. I prefer a flexible work schedule. ....1 2 3 4 5 N/A
3. I let the paraeducator know exactly what is expected. ....1 2 3 4 5 N/A
4. I provide (or at least determine) all the materials that will be used. ....1 2 3 4 5 N/A
5. I provide a written work schedule..1 2 3 4 5 N/A

PTR Paraeducator Work Style Survey—Sample

        Disagree Agree

1. I like to be supervised closely...1 2 3 4 5 N/A
2. I prefer a flexible work schedule. ....1 2 3 4 5 N/A
3. I like to know exactly what is expected. ....1 2 3 4 5 N/A
4. I prefer to decide which materials to use. ....1 2 3 4 5 N/A
5. I prefer to have a written work schedule. ....1 2 3 4 5 N/A

Figure 2.1. Work style survey for teachers and paraeducators (see Appendixes 2.2 and 2.3). (From MANAGING PARAEDUCATORS IN YOUR SCHOOL by N.K. French Copyright 2009 Reproduced with permission of SAGE PUBLICATIONS INC BOOKS in the format Textbook via Copyright Clearance Center.)

answers to these two questions. With respect to supervision, the teacher and paraeducator will need to come to an agreement on the level or type of supervision that will meet both their needs. They will also want to determine the best way to address problematic activities or situations within the classroom so they are able to maintain an open, positive avenue for communication and the teaching environment remains optimal for all students.

TIP

Sometimes team members feel that working on team logistics and work styles is not a top priority. PTR, however, assumes that teams are properly constituted, have committed members, and are based on an understanding and respect for individual team members.

Although questions 1 and 17 demonstrate sharp contrasts between the teacher's and paraeducator's responses, their answers to questions 9 and 13 are strikingly similar. In question 9, both the teacher and paraeducator are comfortable with not giving or receiving specific details on how to complete a task. Thus, it appears that they are somewhat flexible and able to respond spontaneously based upon the need. However, both team members indicate in question 13 that punctuality is extremely important. The responses to these questions demonstrate points of compatibility between the teacher and paraeducator.

Paraeducator		Teacher
Disagree Agree	**Item Content**	**Disagree Agree**
①2 3 4 5 N/A.............................1. Closeness of supervision. ....1 2 3④5 N/A
①2 3 4 5 N/A.............................9. Specifying how to do each task...................................1②3 4 5 N/A
①2 3 4 5 N/A.............................12. Taking care of details. 1 2 3 4⑤N/A
1 2 3 4⑤N/A.............................13. Punctuality...1 2 3 4⑤N/A
①2 3 4 5 N/A.............................17. Discussing activities that do not go well.....................1 2 3 4⑤N/A

Figure 2.2. Work style score comparison between teacher and paraeducator (see Appendix 2.4). (From MANAGING PARAEDUCATORS IN YOUR SCHOOL by N.K. French Copyright 2009 Reproduced with permission of SAGE PUBLICATIONS INC BOOKS in the format Textbook via Copyright Clearance Center.)

Finally, the responses to question 12 from the teacher and paraeducator are completely opposite. However, this discrepancy does not necessarily indicate either a strength or a weakness, but simply a difference in abilities. By knowing this information, the teacher is able to adjust expectations. The teacher may also begin teaching the needed skills to the paraprofessional for increasing his or her ability to attend to task details. As these examples demonstrate, the work style survey provides the team with an objective starting point from which to address similarities and differences, as well as strengths and weaknesses, between teachers and paraeducators. This information will result in increased open communication and trust between these particular team members, as well as an enhanced overall teaming process.

Communication: Data-Based Decision Making and Consensus

Although it is important to understand the supervision and work style preferences of fellow team members, knowing how to make decisions and gain consensus as a team is also essential. To move through each step in the PTR model, the team will need to develop an effective method for sharing ideas, addressing concerns, answering questions, and determining priorities. Developing an effective communication system among the team may involve altering how members approach this process. PTR is a data-driven model; as such, it uses data to answer questions, address concerns, and generate solutions. Because an important task for each team is to create and maintain an effective communication system that uses the data to make decisions, team meetings should be structured as follows:

1. Review all available and pertinent data

2. Brainstorm ideas based on the data

3. Discuss, prioritize, and make data-based decisions

4. Gain consensus and implement agreed upon steps

The first task of each meeting is to discuss the available data regarding the student of concern. The team should collect initial baseline data and then continue to collect additional data throughout the PTR process. The data should be used to inform and guide the team's discussions and brainstorming sessions. As discussed in Chapter 3, the team should use the current data to discuss the most significant behaviors of concern, as well as the potential goals for the student. The data used during this initial discussion may include information from the student's individualized education program if the student is in special education, formal or informal data measures previously or currently being used with the student, parent reports, or any other pertinent data available to the team.

Once the data are reviewed by the team, the next task is to use that information to answer questions and address team members' concerns. Brainstorming is an efficient and effective way to achieve this goal. At the start of the session, members should be encouraged to share their viewpoints and knowledge, based on their disciplines, in response to the questions or concerns generated by the data. Remember, all ideas should be considered and criticizing the statements of others should not be permissible. A "round robin" approach is one way to get input from all team members in a trusting environment. This approach requires each team member to think about responses to issues presented by a facilitator and write them down on paper or a card. When it is time to share ideas, the facilitator asks each team member to offer one of the ideas he or she wrote. The team members continue to offer their ideas until they have exhausted all that had been written. At this point, the team can ask clarifying questions about the ideas offered by others. Finally, the facilitator asks team members to prioritize independently the ideas offered. This can be done by rank-ordering the top three or five ideas on a voting sheet and then summarizing the results. Brainstorming works best in a trusting, accepting environment. If team members feel free to openly ask questions and develop ideas without fear of criticism or judgment, they tend to produce more creative solutions, which results in greater positive outcomes for the student.

Within the PTR model, the team should discuss and make decisions about several important aspects in the process. For example, the team may determine the student's most significant challenging behavior(s), develop specific goals targeted for behavior change, establish a function-based hypothesis regarding the challenging behavior, and select appropriate strategies for the student's intervention plan. This step allows the team to make decisions regarding each of these essential elements within the PTR model based on the data.

The final task within each meeting is to obtain consensus among the members regarding the decisions made and the upcoming steps to be implemented. It is essential to obtain general agreement regarding the results of each meeting prior to moving forward. With consensus, all team members should be able to live with and follow through with the decisions. Achieving such consensus requires input from every team member as each member will be involved at some level in the final outcomes. Although the PTR model is a team-driven process, the classroom teacher most often serves as the primary intervention agent. Therefore, it is essential to fully consider the teacher's input and preferences during every aspect of the process.

TIP   *In team meetings, members should review data, brainstorm ideas, make data-based decisions, and gain consensus.*

Developing an effective intervention plan requires teaming, collaboration, data-based decision making, and consensus. When teams are inconsistent in any of these areas, even the most powerful and well-designed intervention plan may not be as successful as desired. However, when teams use effective teaming and communication systems, collect and use data to make informed decisions, and gain group consensus regarding next steps to be implemented, the behavior intervention plan usually results in positive and appropriate outcomes for the student.

ROLES AND RESPONSIBILITIES

The final critical component to effective teaming entails the clear delineation of roles and responsibilities. Defining team member roles and responsibilities begins in the initial meeting and carries through to behavior plan implementation and evaluation within the classroom. Most teams have a limited amount of time allotted for planning. By establishing precise roles and responsibilities at the onset, meetings become less time consuming, content remains focused, and identifiable outcomes are obtainable, resulting in more pertinent and meaningful experiences for all team members.

The first step toward ensuring effective use of time and obtaining identifiable outcomes is through the development of a short, succinct action plan during each meeting. The action plan includes tasks to be completed prior to the next meeting (e.g., gather data, review interventions, plan implementation), as well as the specific responsibilities assigned to each team member (e.g., collect data, make materials, speak with the administrator, contact the speech therapist). Creating an action plan ensures that there will be follow-through on the ideas generated during the meeting and that tasks will be completed between sessions. Roles, which should be defined and/or assigned to ensure meetings proceed as efficiently and effectively as possible, include the following:

- Facilitator
- Developer of the next meeting's agenda

- Action plan recorder
- Time keeper

The facilitator is responsible for keeping the team focused on the agenda and ensuring that all items are covered. The facilitator may be a different team member from meeting to meeting, depending on the needs and desires of the team. Often, the facilitator will be the team member with the greatest knowledge and experience about behavioral principles and positive behavior support, along with training in the development and implementation of effective intervention strategies (i.e., the school psychologist, behavior analyst, or behavior specialist). Regardless of who is chosen, it is important that the facilitator maintains a positive and open atmosphere, keeps the discussion focused on data and factual information, and strives to develop a realistic action plan as the final goal of the meeting.

At the end of each meeting, the team may choose to select a member to develop an agenda for the next meeting. A written agenda keeps the team focused and allows for optimal use of time. The team may briefly review what items should be included on the next meeting's agenda. If possible, the final agenda should be sent to all the team members at least a day prior to the meeting. Typically, the development of the agenda is included in the facilitator's responsibilities, but each team has the flexibility to make this determination depending on their team's composition.

The action plan recorder is responsible for documenting the steps to be taken by each team member prior to the next meeting, as determined by the team. The action plan includes the tasks to be completed, the team member responsible for each task, and the specific dates or timeline for the completion of each activity. The recorder is also responsible for ensuring that each team member knows and understands his or her individual responsibilities. Ideally, the recorder provides each team member with a copy of the action plan within a day of the meeting.

Depending on the size and makeup of the team, a specific individual may be designated as the time keeper. However, this responsibility may also fall to the facilitator. This person will keep the team on track throughout the meeting and ensure that all items on the agenda are addressed in a timely manner. It is imperative that the other team members respect the time keeper's prompts to move on and keep to the prearranged schedule.

SUMMARY

The PTR model uses meetings to develop goals, gather and summarize information, determine the function of the student's challenging behavior, design intervention plans, and evaluate outcome data. Every meeting has a specific purpose and the information gathered and discussed during each meeting is applicable to the next steps in the process. One of the primary goals of the teaming process is to create a feeling of accomplishment. Then, the meetings take on greater meaning for the team and members are willing to expend the time and energy to achieve the desired outcome for the student.

No predetermined number of meetings is required for the PTR model. The number of meetings and the time spent on each step is a function of the complexity of the case and the challenges involved in arranging and delivering intervention. Depending on the complexity and the goals of the group, each team may proceed through the process using its own time frame. For example, a small team consisting of only the classroom teacher and behavior specialist may choose to complete the process in two or three meetings by covering multiple steps during each session. A larger team of five or six members may choose to complete only one step during each meeting. Ultimately, the teaming process within the PTR model allows the team the flexibility to structure their meetings to ensure the most effective and efficient use of the team's time and resources.

Appendix

2

PTR Classroom Team Survey

School _____   Name _____

Directions: Complete this survey if the team meets regularly for planning purposes. Circle the applicable number for each statement, then complete the questions that follow.

1. Our team meets for planning purposes.

Rarely/never	Monthly	Bimonthly	Weekly	Daily
0	1	2	3	4

2. Our team plans daily classroom activities collaboratively.

Rarely	Occasionally	Frequently	Usually	Almost always
0	1	2	3	4

3. Our team plans collaboratively around implementing individualized education program objectives and making adaptations and modifications for the students.

Rarely	Occasionally	Frequently	Usually	Almost always
0	1	2	3	4

4. Our team communicates well and problem solves collaboratively.

Strongly disagree	Disagree	Neutral	Agree	Strongly agree
0	1	2	3	4

5. Our team interacts and works with children across developmental domains and disciplines.

Rarely	Occasionally	Frequently	Usually	Almost always
0	1	2	3	4

6. Professional roles and responsibilities are shared across team members.

Strongly disagree	Disagree	Neutral	Agree	Strongly agree
0	1	2	3	4

7. Parents play an active role on their child's team regarding the identification of goals, supports and services, modifications and adaptations.

Strongly disagree	Disagree	Neutral	Agree	Strongly agree
0	1	2	3	4

8. Our team has access to additional resources to help us work with students in the classroom (e.g., technology, personnel, classroom materials).

None	Limited	Adequate	Good	Excellent
0	1	2	3	4

Please answer the following questions:

1. What are some strengths of the team?

2. What challenges face the team?

3. What are the most pressing needs of the team?

4. What might help to enhance the team's productivity?

PTR Teacher Work Style Survey

Directions: Circle the number that indicates your level of agreement or disagreement with each statement.

	Disagree Agree
1. I like to supervise paraeducators closely.	1 2 3 4 5 N/A
2. I prefer a flexible work schedule.	1 2 3 4 5 N/A
3. I let paraeducators know exactly what is expected.	1 2 3 4 5 N/A
4. I provide (or at least determine) all the materials that will be used.	1 2 3 4 5 N/A
5. I provide a written work schedule.	1 2 3 4 5 N/A
6. I expect the paraeducator to think ahead to the next task.	1 2 3 4 5 N/A
7. I determine the instructional methods that will be used.	1 2 3 4 5 N/A
8. I encourage the paraeducator to try new activities independently.	1 2 3 4 5 N/A
9. I give explicit directions for each task.	1 2 3 4 5 N/A
10. I always do several things at one time.	1 2 3 4 5 N/A
11. I like working with paraeducators that willingly take on new challenges.	1 2 3 4 5 N/A
12. I like taking care of details.	1 2 3 4 5 N/A
13. I require the paraeducator to be punctual.	1 2 3 4 5 N/A
14. I like to get feedback on how I can improve as a supervisor.	1 2 3 4 5 N/A
15. I like to bring problems out in the open.	1 2 3 4 5 N/A
16. I like to give frequent performance feedback to the paraeducator.	1 2 3 4 5 N/A
17. I like to discuss activities that do not go well.	1 2 3 4 5 N/A
18. I like working with other adults.	1 2 3 4 5 N/A
19. I encourage paraeducators to think for themselves.	1 2 3 4 5 N/A
20. I am a morning person.	1 2 3 4 5 N/A
21. I speak slowly and softly.	1 2 3 4 5 N/A
22. I work best alone with little immediate interaction.	1 2 3 4 5 N/A
23. I need a quiet place to work without distractions.	1 2 3 4 5 N/A
24. I prefer that no one else touches my things.	1 2 3 4 5 N/A
25. I prefer to work from a written plan.	1 2 3 4 5 N/A

Adapted from MANAGING PARAEDUCATORS IN YOUR SCHOOL by N.K. French Copyright 2009 Reproduced with permission of SAGE PUBLICATIONS INC BOOKS in the format Textbook via Copyright Clearance Center.

In *Prevent-Teach-Reinforce: The School-Based Model of Individualized Positive Behavior Support* by G. Dunlap, R. Iovannone, D. Kincaid, K. Wilson, K. Christiansen, P. Strain, and C. English. (2010, Paul H. Brookes Publishing Co., Inc.)

PTR Paraeducator Work Style Survey

Directions: Circle the number that indicates your level of agreement or disagreement with each statement.

		Disagree				**Agree**	
1.	I like to be supervised closely.	1	2	3	4	5	N/A
2.	I like a flexible work schedule.	1	2	3	4	5	N/A
3.	I like to know exactly what is expected.	1	2	3	4	5	N/A
4.	I prefer to decide which materials to use.	1	2	3	4	5	N/A
5.	I like having a written work schedule.	1	2	3	4	5	N/A
6.	I need time to think ahead on the next task.	1	2	3	4	5	N/A
7.	I like to determine the instructional methods I use.	1	2	3	4	5	N/A
8.	I like to try new activities independently.	1	2	3	4	5	N/A
9.	I like to be told how to do each task.	1	2	3	4	5	N/A
10.	I like to do several things at one time.	1	2	3	4	5	N/A
11.	I like to take on challenges and new situations.	1	2	3	4	5	N/A
12.	I like taking care of details.	1	2	3	4	5	N/A
13.	I like to be very punctual.	1	2	3	4	5	N/A
14.	I like to give frequent feedback on how I prefer to be supervised.	1	2	3	4	5	N/A
15.	I like to bring problems out in the open.	1	2	3	4	5	N/A
16.	I like to get frequent feedback on my performance.	1	2	3	4	5	N/A
17.	I like to discuss when activities do not go well.	1	2	3	4	5	N/A
18.	I like working with other adults.	1	2	3	4	5	N/A
19.	I like to think things through for myself.	1	2	3	4	5	N/A
20.	I am a morning person.	1	2	3	4	5	N/A
21.	I like to speak slowly and softly.	1	2	3	4	5	N/A
22.	I like to work alone with little immediate interaction.	1	2	3	4	5	N/A
23.	I need a quiet place to work without distractions.	1	2	3	4	5	N/A
24.	I prefer that no one else touches my things.	1	2	3	4	5	N/A
25.	I prefer to work from a written plan.	1	2	3	4	5	N/A

In *Prevent-Teach-Reinforce: The School-Based Model of Individualized Positive Behavior Support* by G. Dunlap, R. Iovannone, D. Kincaid, K. Wilson, K. Christiansen, P. Strain, and C. English. (2010, Paul H. Brookes Publishing Co., Inc.)

PTR Work Style Score Comparison Sheet

Directions: Transfer scores from the PTR Teacher Work Style Survey (Appendix 2.2) and PTR Paraeducator Work Style Survey (Appendix 2.3) to this form. Look for areas of agreement and disagreement. However, there are no right or wrong responses. Determine areas of concern and solutions in light of the areas of agreement and disagreement.

Paraeducator		Item Content	Teacher	
Disagree Agree			**Disagree**	**Agree**
1 2 3 4 5 N/A	....	1. Closeness of supervision.	.........1 2 3 4 5 N/A	
1 2 3 4 5 N/A	....	2. Flexibility of work schedule.	.........1 2 3 4 5 N/A	
1 2 3 4 5 N/A	....	3. Preciseness of expectations.	.........1 2 3 4 5 N/A	
1 2 3 4 5 N/A	....	4. Decisions on materials to use.	.........1 2 3 4 5 N/A	
1 2 3 4 5 N/A	....	5. Written work schedule.	.........1 2 3 4 5 N/A	
1 2 3 4 5 N/A	....	6. Time to think ahead.	.........1 2 3 4 5 N/A	
1 2 3 4 5 N/A	....	7. Decisions on instructional methods.	.........1 2 3 4 5 N/A	
1 2 3 4 5 N/A	....	8. Trying new activities independently.	.........1 2 3 4 5 N/A	
1 2 3 4 5 N/A	....	9. Specifying how to do each task.	.........1 2 3 4 5 N/A	
1 2 3 4 5 N/A	....	10. Doing several things at one time.	.........1 2 3 4 5 N/A	
1 2 3 4 5 N/A	....	11. Taking on challenges.	.........1 2 3 4 5 N/A	
1 2 3 4 5 N/A	....	12. Taking care of details.	.........1 2 3 4 5 N/A	
1 2 3 4 5 N/A	....	13. Punctuality.	.........1 2 3 4 5 N/A	
1 2 3 4 5 N/A	....	14. Giving/getting feedback on supervision.	.........1 2 3 4 5 N/A	
1 2 3 4 5 N/A	....	15. Dealing with problems out in the open.	.........1 2 3 4 5 N/A	
1 2 3 4 5 N/A	....	16. Giving/getting feedback.	.........1 2 3 4 5 N/A	
1 2 3 4 5 N/A	....	17. Discussing activities that do not go well.	.........1 2 3 4 5 N/A	
1 2 3 4 5 N/A	....	18. Working with other adults.	.........1 2 3 4 5 N/A	
1 2 3 4 5 N/A	....	19. Thinking things through for myself.	.........1 2 3 4 5 N/A	
1 2 3 4 5 N/A	....	20. Morning person.	.........1 2 3 4 5 N/A	
1 2 3 4 5 N/A	....	21. Speak slowly and softly.	.........1 2 3 4 5 N/A	
1 2 3 4 5 N/A	....	22. Working alone—little interaction.	.........1 2 3 4 5 N/A	
1 2 3 4 5 N/A	....	23. Quiet place to work/no distractions.	.........1 2 3 4 5 N/A	
1 2 3 4 5 N/A	....	24. Touching others' things.	.........1 2 3 4 5 N/A	
1 2 3 4 5 N/A	....	25. Working from a written plan.	.........1 2 3 4 5 N/A	

In *Prevent-Teach-Reinforce: The School-Based Model of Individualized Positive Behavior Support* by G. Dunlap, R. Iovannone, D. Kincaid, K. Wilson, K. Christiansen, P. Strain, and C. English. (2010, Paul H. Brookes Publishing Co., Inc.)

Goal Setting and Data Collection

3

OVERVIEW AND OBJECTIVES

The goal-setting step of the Prevent-Teach-Reinforce (PTR) model identifies the team's vision or broad goals for the student and leads to the expansion of specific short-term goals to be targeted for intervention. Once the goals have been established, data collection should begin with the behavior rating scale (BRS), an efficient, easy-to-use tool that is developed by the team. The formation of specific behavioral, social, and/or academic goals highlights the areas for behavior change and provides the team with a point of focus. The data collection system allows for continuous monitoring and evaluation of the student's progress toward achieving those goals.

Chapter 3 focuses on the following objectives:

- Identifying broad goals for the student

- Developing short-term goals based on the broad goals

- Identifying and operationalizing target behavior(s)

- Establishing a daily data collection system to track target behavior(s)

In achieving the objectives of this chapter, the following forms may be helpful: PTR Goal-Setting Form and the BRS (see Appendixes 3.1 and 3.2, respectively). Blank copies of these forms are also included on the accompanying CD.

DEVELOPING BROAD GOALS

The primary purpose of the goal-setting step is to identify the challenging behaviors exhibited by the student that are of greatest concern to the team. To determine the student's short-term goals, each team member should first think about any visions and hopes for the student that can be achieved through the PTR process. Teams that are in agreement on the vision or broad goals for the student tend to be more effective in implementing interventions that are long-lasting and result in meaningful change.

If the student is receiving support through special education services, the team's vision or broad goals might be similar to the annual goals for behavior or social relationships listed in the student's individualized education program (IEP). The student's broad goals should target outcomes that transfer across environments and people and lead to a higher quality of life. These broad goals may include

- Behavioral outcomes

- Social interactions or relationships

- Behavior changes necessary for academic achievement

The following examples may assist the team in conceptualizing a broad goal for each of the areas listed above.

Broad Behavioral Goal Example

A team is meeting about a student named Johnny, who engages in tantrums. During the initial brainstorming session, the team members discuss when, where, and how often the tantrums occur. They determine that Johnny engages in the disruptive behaviors numerous times throughout the day. They also agree that a tantrum includes screaming, kicking, and throwing objects and is extremely disruptive to the other students and the teaching environment.

Once the team members determine that the most significant behavior of concern is Johnny's tantrums, they discuss what behaviors they would like to see Johnny demonstrate in place of the tantrums. Again, the team members begin to brainstorm ideas. Some of their suggestions include Johnny raising his hand to request assistance, using an inside voice, or asking a peer for help. The team members agree that the appropriate behaviors are communicative in nature; therefore, they reach consensus on the following broad behavioral goal: *Johnny will communicate his wants and needs in an age-appropriate manner.*

Broad Social Goal Example

During their discussion, several team members mention concerns about Johnny's peer relationships. Specifically, team members note that most of the students in the classroom do not choose to interact with Johnny. After brainstorming ideas, the team members decide that Johnny would benefit from having a broad goal to address his peer relationships. They reach consensus on the following broad goal: *Johnny will demonstrate appropriate social skills to maintain friends.*

TIP *For many teams, the development of broad goals represents a critical perspective shift. In developing broad goals, the team members no longer view their sole job as stopping a student's challenging behavior.*

Broad Academic Goal Example

The teacher now addresses personal concerns regarding Johnny's lack of academic progress due to his numerous daily tantrums. The team members review all the information available to them with respect to Johnny's academic situation. They agree that Johnny is often off task and does not complete many assignments. After gaining consensus, the team members agree on the following broad academic goal: *Johnny will increase task engagement during academic tasks.*

Each of these broad goal examples target future outcomes that transfer across people, situations, and environments and will ultimately lead to a higher quality of life for the student. These broad goals will be the foundation for developing the student's short-term goals, which is the next activity in the goal-setting step of the PTR process.

DEVELOPING SHORT-TERM GOALS

Once the broad goals have been established, the team should use them as the foundation for developing the student's short-term goals. Short-term goals are the specific behavior, social, and/or academic changes that need to occur to achieve the broad goals. Some short-term goals may already be established for a student receiving special education services through an IEP. If the student has an IEP, it may be helpful for the team to review those goals at this time. However, the team may agree to develop short-term goals independent of the student's IEP.

The following areas are addressed within the short-term goals:

- Decrease specific challenging behaviors (i.e., problem, social, and academic behaviors) demonstrated by the student that are of greatest concern to the team and prevent the student from reaching the broad goals.

- Increase appropriate replacement behavior(s) to be demonstrated by the student in place of the challenging behavior in the three categories (i.e., problem, social, academic) that will enable the student to reach the broad goals.

It is vital to develop specific, clearly defined short-term goals. A well-developed operational definition of each short-term goal facilitates communication among the team members involved in the intervention process and allows for more accurate and reliable data collection.

In the previous example, the team members expressed concerns about Johnny's daily tantrums and how those behaviors appeared to significantly affect other aspects of his life, such as his peer relationships and academic achievement. The team members then agreed that Johnny's broad behavioral goal would be to communicate his wants and needs in an age-appropriate manner. To achieve this outcome, the team members must now determine the short-term goals for Johnny. The short-term goals should define the specific challenging behaviors that need to decrease, as well as the behavior the team would like to see Johnny demonstrate instead of the challenging behavior (i.e., desired replacement behavior). The team members may begin by asking the following (or similar) questions:

1. How does Johnny currently communicate his wants and needs? (*Answer:* He engages in tantrums that disrupt the classroom.)

2. What challenging behaviors does he display instead of communicating effectively? (*Answer:* He calls and/or talks out, screams, bangs his desk, kicks, and throws things.)

3. What are the specific behaviors Johnny engages in that are most problematic? (*Answer:* Screaming, kicking his desk or those nearby, and throwing materials.)

4. Do these challenging behaviors have a significant impact on his quality of life? On the learning environment? On other students? (*Answer:* Johnny is often removed from the room and isolated from his peers. His behavior is extremely disruptive to the teaching/learning environment. His peers avoid him, resulting in limited positive peer interactions.)

5. What behavior(s) would be more appropriate for Johnny to demonstrate to express his wants and needs instead of the challenging behavior? (*Answer:* Using an inside voice and keeping his body calm without throwing things.)

6. How do other students his age appropriately communicate their wants and needs? (*Answer:* Raise their hand, use a normal, inside tone of voice, sit quietly, and wait for teacher assistance.)

7. Are their wants and needs met using these methods? (*Answer:* Yes, most of the time.)

8. Does Johnny have the skills in his repertoire to use these methods? (*Answer:* Johnny has the skills needed to raise his hand to request help.)

TIP *A good short-term goal is one that all team members are enthusiastic about achieving.*

After discussing each of these (or similar) questions and sharing ideas regarding Johnny's tantrums, the team members agree on the following short-term behavioral goals:

1. Johnny will decrease screaming, kicking furniture and/or people, and throwing objects to express his wants and needs.

2. Johnny will verbally express his wants and needs in the classroom by raising his hand, using an inside voice, and keeping his body calm (i.e., desired replacement behavior).

Once consensus has been achieved regarding the student's short-term behavioral goals, the team should follow the same question-and-answer procedure to develop the student's social and academic short-term goals. It is important for the team to remain focused on those behaviors exhibited by the student that are of greatest concern, as well as how those behaviors influence the student's social interactions and academic progress.

Continuing with the example, Johnny's team determined that the most significant concern was the tantrum behavior. The team members agreed that Johnny should communicate his wants and needs in an age-appropriate manner. They also expressed concerns that Johnny's tantrums may be contributing to his poor peer interactions and social isolation. Therefore, the team determined that Johnny's broad social goal will be to demonstrate appropriate social skills to gain and maintain friends. To accomplish this outcome, the team may consider the following (or similar) questions when developing the short-term social goals for Johnny:

1. What types of positive interactions are currently occurring between Johnny and his peers? (*Answer:* Brief social interactions such as "Hi," "What's up?," or "Want to play?")

2. How often do peers ask Johnny to join in group interactions? (*Answer:* Occasionally, but less often as the year has progressed.)

3. How does Johnny usually respond to his peers during play? (*Answer:* Usually in a positive, appropriate manner.)

4. How often do peers choose Johnny as a work buddy? (*Answer:* Rarely. Student reports indicate that peers do not want to work with Johnny because he screams, throws things, and kicks.)

5. How does Johnny respond to peers during academic work groups? (*Answer:* Sometimes he is able to interact in an appropriate manner, but often he appears to be easily frustrated and engages in screaming and other behavioral outbursts such as tantrums.)

6. What impact does the challenging behavior (tantrums) have on Johnny's peer relationships? (*Answer:* Other students do not want to work with Johnny and often complain about having him in their work group.)

Based on group discussion and answers to the questions above, the team developed the following short-term social goals:

1. Johnny will reduce the number of times he screams at and/or throws objects toward other children during group assignments.

2. Johnny will use a calm and normal tone of voice when interacting with his peers during academic work groups (i.e., prosocial replacement behavior).

Finally, the team should develop short-term academic goals for the student using the broad goal that was agreed on earlier during the initial brainstorming session. The team should address questions regarding how the student's behavior of concern may be impacting his or her academic progress. In the example of Johnny, the team agreed that his broad academic goal was to increase task engagement time during academic activities. To attain this outcome, the team may want to address the following (or similar) questions:

1. Does the student engage in the challenging behavior(s) during academic work sessions? (*Answer:* Yes.)

2. Is the behavior more problematic during independent or group work? (*Answer:* During both.)

3. Does the challenging behavior impede the student's ability to succeed academically? (*Answer:* Yes, when he is not engaged, he does not complete his tasks.)

4. Does the student possess the skills to engage in more appropriate behavior(s) during academic activities? (*Answer:* He stays engaged in tasks he likes to do, such as working on the computer.)

5. What behavior(s) would the student need to exhibit in place of the challenging behavior to be more successful academically within the classroom? (*Answer:* Staying engaged in a task until it is completed.)

By asking these questions, the team will be able to develop short-term academic goals for the student. Once Johnny's team addressed these questions, they developed the following short-term academic goals:

1. Johnny will decrease screaming and throwing work materials during academic activities.

2. Johnny will increase the amount of time he remains calm in his seat, with his eyes focused on the teacher or work materials during academic assignments (i.e., appropriate replacement behavior).

> **TIP**
>
> *Short-term goals focus on two areas: the specific challenging behavior(s) to be decreased and the appropriate behavior the student should demonstrate in lieu of the challenging behavior (i.e., desired replacement behavior). Teams always should include both in the PTR process.*

The team's completed PTR Goal-Setting Form is provided in Figure 3.1. The team must remain focused on the primary purpose of the goal-setting step. The intention of this step is to identify the challenging behaviors exhibited by the student that are of greatest concern to the team. When determining the student's short-term goals, team members should first think about their visions for the student and what the student will achieve through this process. Short-term goals are the specific behavioral, social, and/or academic outcomes that need to occur to achieve the broad goals. Well-defined operational definitions of each short-term goal facilitate communication among team members, allow for more accurate and reliable data collection, set the stage for more effective intervention implementation, and assist the team in attaining results with meaningful change.

DATA COLLECTION

After the team has identified and gained consensus on the behavioral, social, and academic short-term goals for the student, they should develop a system for collecting data on the behaviors addressed within the goals. The data obtained throughout baseline and intervention will be essential to the team in making appropriate decisions when completing the functional behavior assessment (FBA) and developing the behavior intervention plan. The team should be able to answer the following questions using the data collected:

Directions:

1. Identify one broad goal in each category.
2. Under each broad goal, identify the behavior(s) to be decreased and the prosocial behavior(s) to be increased to achieve the broad goal.
3. Clearly define or operationalize the goals so that each goal is
   a. Observable (seen or heard)
   b. Measurable (counted or timed)
   c. Significant (impact on student's life)

Example: Goals for Johnny

	Behavioral goal	**Social goal**	**Academic goal**
Broad goals	Johnny will communicate his wants and needs in an age-appropriate manner.	Johnny will demonstrate age-appropriate social skills to maintain friends.	Johnny will increase task engagement time during academic activities.
Short-term goals decrease	Johnny will decrease screaming, kicking furniture and/or people, and throwing objects to express his wants and needs.	Johnny will reduce the number of times he screams at and/or throws objects toward other children during group assignments.	Johnny will decrease screaming and throwing work materials during academic activities.
Short-term goals increase	Johnny will verbally express his wants and needs in the classroom by using an inside voice and calm body.	Johnny will use a calm, normal tone of voice when interacting with his peers during academic work groups.	Johnny will increase the amount of time he remains in his seat with eyes focused on the teacher and/or work materials during academic assignments.

Figure 3.1.   An example of a completed Goal-Setting Form (see Appendix 3.1).

1. Is the student's challenging behavior one that should be targeted for intervention?
2. Are the intervention strategies effective in decreasing the student's challenging behavior after implementation?
3. Is the student increasing the use of the replacement behavior?
4. Are the goals of the intervention being met?
5. Are modifications needed to the intervention plan? If so, what types of modifications need to be made?

One simple tool for collecting data is the behavior rating scale (BRS) (cf. Kohler & Strain, 1992), a 5-point measure used in the PTR model to facilitate daily collection of the student's targeted behaviors. The BRS consists of detailed behavior anchors that are defined by the team. It is a perceptual scale and does not require the teacher to tally, count, or use a stop-watch to time behavior. Rather, once the behaviors are defined and the anchors set, the teacher (or any other intervention agent) simply rates the performance of the behavior by circling the anchor that most closely corresponds with his or her perception. An example of a completed BRS is provided in Figure 3.1. The BRS is a key component in the PTR process and serves as the tool to quantify the targeted behavior(s).

Collecting BRS data allows the team to compare the behavior(s) across contexts, identify behavioral trends, and evaluate the effectiveness of the intervention strategies once the behavior plan has been developed and implemented. The BRS should be used throughout the PTR process (baseline and intervention implementation) to measure the increase and/or decrease of targeted behaviors.

Three key areas should be addressed when developing the BRS:

1. Defining the target behavior(s) so that it is measurable and observable

2. Determining the best method (i.e., scale) for measuring the target behavior(s)

3. Establishing appropriate anchor points for recording behavioral occurrence

All of these elements are essential for accurately measuring behavior change.

Defining Target Behaviors

The first step in the development of the BRS is to determine appropriate operational definitions for each behavior the team wants to track (i.e., problem, social, and/or academic). The team should clearly describe each behavior, being as specific, objective, and descriptive as possible. The team should use the short-term goals previously developed to create the BRS. Several behaviors of concern probably will be identified by the team as being significant (e.g., tantrums, out of seat, crawling under desks). As the team begins to develop the BRS, it is not necessary to target all challenging behaviors identified in the short-term goals, as this could be quite overwhelming. Instead, the team should prioritize the challenging behaviors and gain consensus regarding which behavior is the most significant, which behavior ranks second, and so forth. The team should select only the top one or two behaviors of concern to track using the BRS, which will help to ensure that the behavior intervention plan developed later focuses on the primary challenging behavior(s), is feasible for the teacher to implement, and allows for obtainable behavior changes for the student.

Returning to the previous example, Johnny's team determined that his daily tantrums were the most significant behaviors of concern. Johnny's short-term behavioral goal was to decrease tantrums. The team members need to agree on an operational definition (i.e., a clearly defined description) of Johnny's tantrums that will allow each member to consistently recognize when Johnny is engaged in a tantrum. The team begins by making a list of all the different behaviors Johnny demonstrates that were of greatest concern to each member. Those behaviors include screaming, repeatedly calling out, kicking furniture, throwing pencils and papers, mumbling, kicking others, and scribbling on his assignments. After discussing all the behaviors, the team members agree that the operational definition of Johnny's tantrums will include screaming, kicking furniture and/or people, and throwing work materials. At minimum, all three behaviors will need to occur to label Johnny's behavior as a tantrum.

In addition, the team members had decided that Johnny's short-term academic goal was to increase academic engagement time. Now, the team first must determine what behaviors indicate that Johnny is academically engaged. Again, the team members list all the behaviors they believe should be present for Johnny to be engaged in an academic task. After discussing the list, the team members agree on an appropriate operational definition for on-task behavior: *Johnny will remain in his seat with his eyes focused on the teacher or work materials during academic activities.*

All teams should develop operational definitions, similar to the examples above, for each behavior they want to track on the BRS. The definitions must be clear and easily understood by each team member. The BRS has a space at the bottom of the page that can be used as a key or legend that will include the operational descriptions developed by the team for each targeted behavior to ensure accuracy of measurement.

Methods of Measurement

After the behaviors are clearly defined, the team needs to determine which metric (e.g., frequency, duration, intensity) is most appropriate for measuring the occurrence of each behavior. This can be determined by asking the team what their greatest concern is about the behavior's occurrence. Is it the number of times the behavior is performed (frequency), how long it lasts (duration), its severity (intensity), or the amount of time it takes for the student to perform the behavior after a request is made (latency)? Once the metric is determined, the anchor points can be set.

Developing Anchor Points

Once the team agrees on the best method (frequency, duration, or intensity) for measuring the targeted behaviors, the next step is to establish appropriate anchor points for the BRS. The process for setting anchors on the BRS is similar across all metrics. When setting anchor points for *challenging behavior*, the first step is to determine the behavior's occurrence on a typical day. This response (e.g., 4–6 times, 10 minutes, 10% of opportunities) becomes Anchor 4. Next, the team discusses the reasonable goal they would like to achieve by the end of the intervention period and sets this as Anchor 1. The team now completes the remainder of the anchor points. Anchor 5 represents a day that is worse than a typical day; therefore, the anchor point will be set at a measure greater than Anchor 4. For example, if the team determines that Jill typically uses curse words in group work about 8–10 times per day (Anchor 4), Anchor 5 would represent Jill having an extremely bad day by cursing more often than usual (i.e., more than 10 times per day). Anchors 3 and 2 will represent intermediate performances between the typical day (Anchor 4) and the reasonable goal (Anchor 1). This can be accomplished by subtracting Anchor 1 from Anchor 4, dividing the difference by 2, and then splitting the difference in half and applying it to Anchors 2 and 3. If ranges are used, the upper range in the reasonable goal would be subtracted from the lower range in the typical day. Consider Jill, who typically curses 8–10 times per day. The team decided that a reasonable goal (Anchor 1) would be 0–2 times per day. If we subtract the upper range of Anchor 1 (2) from the lower range of Anchor 4 (8) and divide the difference by two ($8 - 2 = 6 / 2 = 3$), we can then split the difference between Anchors 3 and 2. Anchor 3 represents 5–7 occurrences of cursing behavior, whereas Anchor 2 represents 3–4 occurrences.

Setting up the BRS anchors for *appropriate behavior* is identical to the challenging behavioral process described above; however, because the team wants to see these behaviors improve (or increase), the scale is reversed. That is, the typical day is set at Anchor 2 (rather than 4), the most undesirable day is set at Anchor point 1 (rather than 5), and the reasonable goal is set at Anchor 5 (rather than 1). The interim anchor points for appropriate behavior are points 2 and 3. Revisiting Jill's case, the team determined that the behavior they would prefer Jill to use in place of cursing is to use suitable or kind words when interacting with peers and adults during group work. They estimated that on a typical day, she performed this skill approximately once or twice. The team set Anchor 2 at 1–2 times. Next, the team determined that increasing Jill's use of kind words to 10 or more times a day would be ideal. Anchor 5 was set at 10 or more times. Anchor 1, representing extremely bad days for Jill using kind words was set at 0 times (lower than the 1–2 times of Anchor 2). Finally, they set Anchors 3 and 4 by subtracting the upper range of Anchor 2 (2) from the lower range of Anchor 5 (10) and splitting the difference between the two anchor points ($10 - 2 = 8 / 2 = 4$). Anchor 3 became 3–6 times, whereas Anchor 4 became 7–9 times.

Frequency Anchor Points

The frequency of a behavior can be measured in several ways: the number of actual occurrences (e.g., 5 times, 6 times), a range (e.g., 10–20 times per day), or a percentage of time

	BEHAVIOR	Date				
Tantrums	10+ daily	5	5	5	5	5
	8–9	4	4	4	4	4
	6–7	3	3	3	3	3
	4–5	2	2	2	2	2
	0–3	1	1	1	1	1

5 = More than 10 times per day (extremely bad day)
4 = Between 8 and 9 times per day (typical day)
3 = Between 6 and 7 times per day
2 = Between 4 and 5 times per day
1 = 0–3 times per day (reasonable goal)

Figure 3.2. Behavior rating scale (BRS) anchor points developed using frequency measurements (see Appendix 3.2).

(e.g., 0–25%) that the behavior occurs. Returning to Johnny's example, after agreeing on his short-term goals, his team begins to develop the BRS by establishing the appropriate anchor points. First, they ask for an estimate of how often Johnny engages in tantrums on a typical day. Using the operational definition of a tantrum as previously developed and agreed on (i.e., screaming, kicking furniture and/or people, and throwing objects to express wants and needs), the team estimated that Johnny engages in tantrums between 8 and 9 times on a typical day, which became Anchor 4. The reasonable goal set by the team was to reduce the tantrums to 3 or fewer times a day (Anchor 1). Ten or more tantrums became Anchor 5, which represents an extremely bad day (worse than a typical day). The difference between the upper range of Anchor 1 and the lower range of Anchor 4 was computed to determine an appropriate measurement range for Anchors 2 and 3 as shown in Figure 3.2.

Some behaviors being evaluated may occur in routines or observational periods that are of various time durations. In these situations, a team may choose to use percentage of opportunities rather than frequency ranges to measure the student's behavior. Using percentage of opportunities gives the data consistency for comparative purposes. For example, Johnny's team identified communicating the need for a break as an appropriate behavior to possibly replace the tantrums. However, the number of times Johnny could use this behavior may vary depending on the number of opportunities or situations triggering the need each day. The team decided to estimate the percentage of opportunities as the metric for Johnny's anchor points by using the same process as described at the beginning of this section. Because this is an appropriate behavior, the typical day estimate is set at Anchor 2 and the reasonable goal is set at Anchor 5. Figure 3.3 shows Johnny's BRS with percentage of opportunity data anchors.

Duration Anchor Points

A team may decide to measure the duration of a targeted behavior rather than the frequency. Duration can be measured in actual time (e.g., 120 minutes), a range of time (e.g.,

	BEHAVIOR	Date				
Tantrums	>40%	5	5	5	5	5
	31–40%	4	4	4	4	4
	21–30%	3	3	3	3	3
	10–20%	2	2	2	2	2
	<10%	1	1	1	1	1

5 = More than 40% of opportunities (reasonable goal)
4 = Between 31% and 40% of opportunities
3 = Between 21% and 30% of opportunities
2 = Between 10% and 20% of opportunities (typical day)
1 = Less than 10% of opportunities

Figure 3.3. Behavior rating scale (BRS) anchor points developed using percentage measurements (see Appendix 3.2).

5 = More than 10
minutes

4 = Between 8 and 10
minutes (typical day)

3 = Between 5 and
7 minutes

2 = Between 2 and 4 min-
utes (better day)

1 = Less than 2 minutes
(exceptional day, goal)

BEHAVIOR		Date				
Tantrums	>10 min	5	5	5	5	5
	8–10min	4	4	4	4	4
	5–7 min	3	3	3	3	3
	2–4 min	2	2	2	2	2
	< 2 min	1	1	1	1	1

Figure 3.4. Behavior rating scale (BRS) anchor points developed using duration measurements (see Appendix 3.2).

10–20 minutes) or the percentage of an activity (e.g., 25% of circle time). The duration estimates are used to determine the BRS anchor points.

Suppose Johnny's team decides to track how long, on average, his tantrums last. The
team determines that on a typical day, his tantrums are probably 8–10 minutes in duration.
They would like to see the tantrums be reduced to less than 2 minutes. Using this information, the team develops the BRS anchor points in Figure 3.4 to record the duration of
Johnny's tantrums.

Intensity Anchor Points

Behavior can also be measured by tracking differences in intensity. Behaviors suitable for
this type of measurement are those that may be acceptable at lesser magnitude. Suppose
Johnny's primary teacher is most concerned about the intensity of his tantrums. When he
engages in tantrums, the sound is so loud it can be heard outside of the classroom. However, Johnny has deficits in communication abilities and uses various levels of vocalizations
for communication. Although the team members would like to eliminate the tantrums, they
feel that initially decreasing their intensity would be a significant improvement. As a group,
the team members begin to operationally define the intensity of Johnny's tantrums by listing the different levels currently observed. The team members agree on the intensity
anchor points in Figure 3.5 for Johnny's tantrums and document them on the BRS.

Latency Anchor Points

If a team is most concerned about the amount of time it takes for a student to respond
after providing an instructional prompt (e.g., take out your books, start working on your
writing assignment), latency would be the most effective measurement. Using the same
process previously described, the team would determine the student's current latency

5 = Ear-piercing (can hear
it on the street)

4 = Louder than play-
ground voice—can
hear it in the parking
lot (typical day)

3 = Playground voice (can
hear it in the next class)

2 = Louder than inside
voice

1 = Soft whimper, squeal

BEHAVIOR		Date				
Screaming	Ear-piercing	5	5	5	5	5
	Louder than playground	4	4	4	4	4
	Playground voice	3	3	3	3	3
	Louder than inside voice	2	2	2	2	2
	Soft whimper/squeal	1	1	1	1	1

Figure 3.5. Behavior rating scale (BRS) anchor points developed using intensity measurements (see Appendix 3.2).

	BEHAVIOR		Date				
		> 6 min.	5	5	5	5	5
Responding to prompts quickly		5–6 min.	4	4	4	4	4
		3–4 min.	3	3	3	3	3
		1–2 min.	2	2	2	2	2
		< 1 min.	1	1	1	1	1

5 = More than 6 minutes elapse between prompt being given and initiation of behavior

4 = 5–6 minutes latency (typical day)

3 = 3–4 minutes latency

2 = 1–2 minutes latency

1 = Less than 1 minute between prompt given and initiation of behavior (reasonable goal)

Figure 3.6. Behavior rating scale (BRS) anchor points developed using latency measurements (see Appendix 3.2).

performance (e.g., 3–5 minutes). They would then agree on a reasonable goal for reducing the time that elapses (e.g., < 1 minute). An example of a BRS using latency anchors is shown in Figure 3.6.

Once the team members gain consensus on how to measure the target behavior(s) and establish the BRS anchor points for recording the behavioral occurrences, they will select a start date for collecting data and identify who will be responsible for completing the BRS. At minimum, the classroom teacher primarily responsible for the student will complete the BRS daily. However, other team members who work with the student on a consistent and/or frequent basis may also record their perceptions using the BRS.

It is important to clarify one point with respect to the development and use of the BRS. It is a flexible tool meant to gather relevant data on challenging behaviors, prosocial behaviors, and replacement behaviors. Because the initial anchor points developed by the team are only estimates or approximations of how often the student engages in each behavior, it is imperative to remember that the team may need to adjust the anchors if it is determined that the original points do not accurately reflect the student's behavior.

For example, Johnny's team initially estimated that he displayed between 7 and 9 tantrums on a typical day (Anchor 4). The team members set a start date and used the BRS to rate Johnny's tantrums for 10 days. At the end of this time period, they met to review the BRS and noted that most of Johnny's tantrum ratings were at Anchor 5 (more than 9 times). In discussion, the team determined that Johnny was not having a continuous period of worse than usual days, but that they had underestimated tantrum occurrence on a typical day. Based on the data reviewed, the team decided to adjust the anchor points as follows:

5 = More than 12 times per day

4 = Between 10 and 12 times per day (typical day)

3 = Between 7 and 9 times per day

2 = Between 4 and 6 times per day

1 = Between 0 and 3 times per day (reasonable goal)

In this example, the BRS data clearly reflect more significant behavior problems than the original estimates. Thus, the team made decisions based on the data from the BRS and changed the anchor points to accurately measure Johnny's daily tantrums.

Not only is a team able to adjust the anchor points for the behaviors initially recorded on the BRS, but they may also add behaviors to the form as needed. At this stage, the team has not yet completed an FBA, developed a function-based hypothesis for the student's challenging behavior, or identified a replacement behavior. For example, Johnny's team initially decided to collect data on his tantrums (problem behavior) and his task engagement time (appropriate academic behavior). However, after the team completed the FBA on Johnny's tantrum behaviors and hypothesized an attention purpose, the team developed a behavior intervention plan (see Chapter 5) to teach Johnny to raise his hand to request help as a replacement behavior for the tantrums. This replacement behavior (hand raising) was not initially identified as a data-tracking behavior on the BRS. However, the team remembered that the BRS is a simple, flexible, easily adjusted tool for daily data collection throughout the PTR process. They decided to start tracking Johnny's hand-raising behavior by operationally defining the new behavior, developing anchor points, and adding it to the BRS.

TIP　　*BRS is most successful when the target behavior is clearly defined, the best method for measuring the behavior(s) is selected, and accurate anchor points are established.*

SUMMARY

When starting the data collection process, the team should have well-defined, operational definitions for each target behavior. Team members will need to decide on the best method for measuring those behaviors by determining what is of most concern. Is it the frequency

Directions:

1. Complete the BRS for each target behavior (problem and prosocial).

2. Operationally define the target behaviors and write the definitions in the key.

3. Determine the best method for measuring the behaviors (i.e., frequency, duration, intensity, latency).

4. Establish appropriate anchor points for recording behavioral occurrence.

5. List the target behaviors on the left side of the form.

6. Determine the start date for collecting data and write it on the form.

7. Determine who will complete the BRS (e.g., the primary teacher will complete the scale, but other team members who see the student on a regular basis and would be able to provide important information may also be included).

8. Complete the BRS at the end of each day, routine, or observational period by circling the number that best corresponds with the rater's perception of the student's behavior for measurement period.

9. Connect the points for each behavior from day to day.

10. The graph will readily provide the team with a visual description of the student's behavioral changes.

EXAMPLE

BEHAVIOR		Date	08/08/08	08/09/08	08/10/08	08/11/08	08/12/08	08/15/08	08/16/08	08/17/08	08/18/08	08/19/08
Task engagement Appropriate behavior	>10 min		5	5	5	5	5	5	5	5	5	5
	8–10 min		4	4	4	4	4	4	4	4	4	4
	5–7 min		3	(3)	(3)	3	3	3	3	3	3	3
	2–4 min		2	2	2	2	2	2	2	2	2	2
	0–1 minute		(1)	1	1	(1)	(1)	1	1	1	1	1
Tantrums Problem behavior	10+daily		(5)	5	5	(5)	5	5	5	5	5	5
	7–9		4	(4)	4	4	(4)	4	4	4	4	4
	4–6		3	3	(3)	3	3	3	3	3	3	3
	2–3		2	2	2	2	2	2	2	2	2	2
	0–1/day		1	1	1	1	1	1	1	1	1	1

Student: _Johnny_　　　　　　　　　School: _____

KEY:

1. **Task engagement:** Rate your perception of the *amount of time* Johnny remains in his seat with eyes focused on the teacher and/or work materials during independent academic work.

2. **Tantrums:** Rate your perception of the *number of times* Johnny engages in screaming, kicking furniture and/or people, and throwing objects (all three behaviors must be present).

Figure 3.7.　An example of a completed behavior rating scale (BRS; see Appendix 3.2).

of occurrence, the amount of time it lasts, the magnitude or intensity of performance, or the amount of time that elapses between a prompt and the initiation of the behavior? Finally, the team will need to establish appropriate anchor points for recording the target behaviors. It is essential for the team to determine the most effective and accurate way to measure and record the student's behavior. The information obtained throughout the data collection process will allow the team to make appropriate decisions when completing the FBA and developing the behavior intervention plan (see Figure 3.7 for an example of a BRS).

Appendix

3

PTR Goal-Setting Form

Directions:

1. Identify one broad goal in each category.
2. Under each broad goal, identify the behavior(s) to be decreased and the prosocial behavior(s) to be increased to achieve the broad goal.
3. Clearly define or operationalize the goals so that each goal is
   a. Observable (seen or heard)
   b. Measurable (counted or timed)
   c. Significant (impact on student's life)

Goals for: _____
(student's name)

	Behavioral	**Social**	**Academic**
Broad goals			
Short-term goals decrease			
Short-term goals increase			

Appendix 3.2.

PTR Behavior Rating Scale

Student _____ School _____

Behavior	Date														
	5 4 3 2 1	5 4 3 2 1	5 4 3 2 1	5 4 3 2 1	5 4 3 2 1	5 4 3 2 1	5 4 3 2 1	5 4 3 2 1	5 4 3 2 1	5 4 3 2 1	5 4 3 2 1	5 4 3 2 1	5 4 3 2 1	5 4 3 2 1	5 4 3 2 1
	5 4 3 2 1	5 4 3 2 1	5 4 3 2 1	5 4 3 2 1	5 4 3 2 1	5 4 3 2 1	5 4 3 2 1	5 4 3 2 1	5 4 3 2 1	5 4 3 2 1	5 4 3 2 1	5 4 3 2 1	5 4 3 2 1	5 4 3 2 1	5 4 3 2 1
	5 4 3 2 1	5 4 3 2 1	5 4 3 2 1	5 4 3 2 1	5 4 3 2 1	5 4 3 2 1	5 4 3 2 1	5 4 3 2 1	5 4 3 2 1	5 4 3 2 1	5 4 3 2 1	5 4 3 2 1	5 4 3 2 1	5 4 3 2 1	5 4 3 2 1
	5 4 3 2 1	5 4 3 2 1	5 4 3 2 1	5 4 3 2 1	5 4 3 2 1	5 4 3 2 1	5 4 3 2 1	5 4 3 2 1	5 4 3 2 1	5 4 3 2 1	5 4 3 2 1	5 4 3 2 1	5 4 3 2 1	5 4 3 2 1	5 4 3 2 1

Prevent-Teach-Reinforce: The School-Based Model of Individualized Positive Behavior Support by G. Dunlap, R. Iovannone, D. Kincaid, K. Wilson, K. Christiansen, P. Strain, and C. English. Copyright © 2010 Paul H. Brookes Publishing Co., Inc. All rights reserved.

39

Functional Behavior Assessment

4

OVERVIEW AND OBJECTIVES

The functional behavior assessment (FBA) step of the Prevent-Teach-Reinforce (PTR) model identifies specific information regarding the student's challenging behavior(s), as well as data relevant to the student's demonstration of appropriate behaviors. The information gathered through the FBA process will help the team to determine the function or purpose of the student's challenging behavior; the antecedents and/or setting events that trigger the inappropriate behaviors; and the people, situations, items, and/or activities that are reinforcing to the student.

The team should complete the FBA Checklist (see Appendix 4.1), which has been developed based on years of research in the field (e.g., Doggett, Edwards, Moore, Tingstrom, & Wilczynski, 2001; Ervin et al., 2001; Hanley, Iwata, & McCord, 2003; Iwata, Dorsey, Slifer, Bauman, & Richman, 1982; Sasso et al., 1992). This information will assist the team in developing the FBA Summary Table (see Appendix 4.2) and ultimately will link the FBA data to the selection of effective and doable Prevent, Teach, and Reinforce strategies for the student's individualized behavior intervention plan.

Chapter 4 focuses on the following objectives:

- Completing the FBA Checklist (Appendix 4.1)

- Developing and analyzing the FBA Summary Table (Appendix 4.2)

- Developing a data-based hypothesis

In achieving the objectives of this chapter, the following forms may be helpful: the FBA Checklist and the FBA Summary Table (see Appendixes 4.1 and 4.2, respectively). Blank copies of these forms are also included on the accompanying CD.

FUNCTIONAL BEHAVIOR ASSESSMENT

The purpose of the FBA step is threefold:

1. To identify the antecedents and/or setting events that trigger the student to engage in challenging behaviors

2. To determine the function or purpose of the student's inappropriate behavior

3. To ascertain the people, situations, items, and/or activities that reinforce the student's behavior

Each of these areas directly relates to one of the components in the PTR model (i.e., Prevent, Teach, Reinforce).

In this section, a sample FBA Checklist is provided for each component. These sample forms were completed in response to the tantrum behavior of a student, Diana.

Note: Functional behavior assessment also is known as "functional assessment" and "functional behavioral assessment."

Diana's team defined tantrums as anytime Diana yelled or screamed and threw objects or hit something. Team members provided input on the definition based on their observations of Diana's tantrum behavior.

TIP   *As teams complete the FBA Checklist, disagreements and different perspectives may emerge. It is best to include all perspectives on the form rather than choose one that is "right."*

Prevent Component

A key scientific principle incorporated within the PTR model is that behavior is influenced by the events and context in which it occurs. Through learning experiences, certain events can trigger challenging behavior, whereas other events may actually prevent challenging behavior from occurring, leading to more appropriate behavioral responses by the student. The prevent component of the FBA identifies both setting events and antecedents that may lead to a student engaging in challenging behavior.

Setting events are those conditions that are separated from the challenging behavior in time and space, including biological or physical conditions (e.g., medication, fatigue, hunger, illness), social events (e.g., fight with parent or sibling, bus difficulties, incarcerated parent), or environmental situations (e.g., noise, lighting, temperature). Examples of setting events include

- A student does not have time to eat breakfast before school and comes to school hungry.

- A student has an argument with a parent before getting on the bus.

Antecedents are distinct people, events, or situations that immediately precede the challenging behavior. Examples of antecedents include

- A student becomes aggressive in the presence of certain peers, but remains calm and appropriate around other peers.

- A student exhibits problem behavior when presented with a nonpreferred task, but immediately begins a highly preferred task without incident.

The primary purpose of the Prevent component is to assist the team with identifying environmental events and circumstances that trigger or contribute to the occurrence of challenging behavior, as well as identifying the situations associated with more desirable prosocial behavior. By accurately identifying both conditions, the team will be able to remove or alter the problematic situations, thus reducing the likelihood of problems occurring while increasing the circumstances that foster appropriate behaviors. When completing the Prevent component of the FBA Checklist, the team should be as specific and accurate as possible with their responses to each question.

In the example of Diana, her team indicated the specific transitions (e.g., the end of art and music classes; transitioning to reading and math classes) that were difficult for Diana, rather than just indicating that transitions are a problem (see question 2a in Figure 4.1). This allowed the team to assess whether the issue was all transitions, or a transition that involved leaving a preferred activity to go to a nonpreferred activity. Note that question 6 was left intentionally blank by the team because none of the events applied to Diana's tantrum behavior. It is important not to leave any items blank unless they truly do not apply to the challenging behavior being assessed. If items are not answered, it would be wise for the team to check with the respondent(s) to make sure that the omission of a response was intended rather than forgotten or skipped.

─────────── PTR FUNCTIONAL BEHAVIOR ASSESSMENT CHECKLIST ───────────

Problem behavior: Tantrums   Person responding: Mrs. Jones (classroom teacher)   Student: Diana

PTR Functional Behavior Assessment	PREVENT Component

1a. Are there *times of the school day* when problem behavior is *most likely* to occur? If yes, what are they?

☒ Morning ☐ Before meals ☐ During meals ☐ After meals ☐ Arrival

☒ Afternoon ☐ Dismissal Other:_____

1b. Are there *times of the school day* when problem behavior is *least likely* to occur? If yes, what are they?

☐ Morning ☐ Before meals ☒ During meals ☐ After meals ☐ Arrival

☐ Afternoon ☐ Dismissal Other:_____

2a. Are there *specific activities* when problem behavior is *very likely* to occur? If yes, what are they?

☒ Reading/LA	☐ Writing	☒ Math	☐ Science
☒ Independent work	☒ Small-group work	☒ Large-group work	☐ Riding the bus
☐ One-on-one	☐ Computer	☐ Recess	☐ Lunch
☐ Free time	☐ Peer/cooperative work	☐ Centers	☐ Discussions/Q&A
☒ Worksheets, seatwork		☐ Specials (specify) _____	☒ Transitions (specify) End of Art & Music; Going to Reading & Math

Other: _____

2b. Are there *specific activities* when cooperative and prosocial behavior is *very likely* to occur? What are they?

☐ Reading/LA	☐ Writing	☐ Math	☒ Science
☐ Independent work	☐ Small-group work	☐ Large-group work	☐ Riding the bus
☐ One-on-one	☒ Computer	☒ Recess	☐ Lunch
☐ Free time	☐ Peer/cooperative work	☐ Centers	☐ Discussions/Q&A
☐ Worksheets, seatwork		☒ Specials (specify) Art & Music	☐ Transitions (specify) _____

Other: _____

3a. Are there *specific classmates or adults* whose proximity is associated with a high likelihood of problem behavior? If so, who are they?

☐ Peers (specify) _____   ☐ Bus driver

☒ Teacher(s) (specify) Mrs. Jones (classroom teacher)   ☐ Parent

☐ Paraprofessional(s) (specify) _____

☒ Other school staff (specify) Ms. Diaz (behavior specialist)

☐ Other family member (specify) _____

Other: _____

3b. Are there *specific classmates or adults* whose proximity is associated with a high likelihood of cooperative and prosocial behavior? If so, who are they?

☐ Peers (specify) _____   ☐ Bus driver

☐ Teacher(s) (specify) _____   ☐ Parent

☐ Paraprofessional(s) (specify) _____

☒ Other school staff (specify) Art teacher, Music teacher, Behavior specialist

☐ Other family member (specify) _____

Other: _____

Figure 4.1. PTR Functional behavior assessment: Prevent component.

(continued)

Figure 4.1. *(continued)*

4. Are there *specific circumstances* that are associated with a high likelihood of problem behavior?

☒ Request to start task ☐ Task too difficult ☒ Transition

☐ Being told work is wrong ☐ Task too long ☐ Student is alone

☒ Reprimand or correction ☒ End of preferred activity ☐ Unstructured time

☒ Told "no" ☐ Task is boring ☐ Novel task

☐ Seated near specific peer ☐ Peer teasing or comments ☐ Change in schedule

☐ Task is repetitive (same task daily) ☐ Removal of preferred item

☒ Start of nonpreferred activity ☐ Down time (no task specified)

☐ Teacher is attending to other students

Other: _____

5. Are there conditions in the *physical environment* that are associated with a high likelihood of problem behavior? For example, too warm or too cold, too crowded, too much noise, too chaotic, weather conditions....

☐ Yes (specify) _____

☒ No

6. Are there circumstances *unrelated to the school setting* that occur on some days and not other days that may make problem behavior more likely?

☐ Illness ☐ No medication ☐ Drug/alcohol abuse

☐ Allergies ☐ Change in medication ☐ Bus conflict

☐ Physical condition ☐ Home conflict ☐ Sleep deprivation

☐ Hunger ☐ Fatigue ☐ Parties or social event

☐ Change in diet ☐ Change in routine ☐ Parent not home

☐ Hormones or menstrual cycle

☐ Stayed with noncustodial parent

Other: _____

Additional comments not addressed above in the *Prevent component:* _____

_____

_____

_____

Teach Component

A second scientific principle incorporated in the FBA process involves how challenging behavior is related to and influenced by circumstances in the environment. A major premise within this perspective is that challenging behavior can be viewed as having a specific purpose or function, which is often communicative in nature. For example, challenging behavior may be exhibited to get attention in the same way as saying "Hey, look at me!" Alternatively, it may serve to escape or avoid something undesired and may communicate the message, "Leave me alone!" Thus, an essential objective of the FBA Checklist is to determine the function of the challenging behavior. This is especially important when the team begins to select interventions or replacement behaviors from the Teach component of the PTR model in the next step of the process. Simply stopping or reducing the occurrence of challenging behavior is often not effective when used in isolation. In an effective intervention plan, the student should be taught a new skill or socially acceptable replacement behavior that serves the same function as the challenging behavior.

The key purpose of the Teach component of the FBA is to assist the team with identifying the function of the challenging behavior (e.g., to get something or someone, to escape or avoid something or someone). When completing the Teach component, the team should respond to all of the items on the checklist that relate to or address the behavior(s) of concern. The team should be as precise as possible by identifying specific situations, people, activities, objects, or items that may apply in each question. Once the purpose of the challenging behavior has been determined, the team will be better equipped to identify effective alternative replacement behaviors to teach the student. The desired alternative behavior should work as effectively and efficiently as the challenging behavior, thus rendering the challenging behavior inadequate for meeting the student's needs.

It is important for the team to identify a replacement behavior that is easy for the student to learn and use, yet is as effective in achieving the student's purpose as the challenging behavior. In addition, the Teach component will aid the team with identifying other behaviors the student should learn in order to improve problem-solving abilities or social interactions. In general, the more the team can expand the student's interpersonal competencies, the more challenging behavior will be reduced.

The checklist completed by Diana's team is provided in Figure 4.2. Diana's team indicated that behaviors appeared to serve multiple purposes, including getting adult attention (classroom teacher and behavior specialist) and escaping or delaying a transition from preferred classes (music and art) to nonpreferred activities (reading and math). Possible replacement skills selected by the team included getting attention appropriately, transitioning without a tantrum from art and music, communicating her emotions, and making appropriate requests. Occasionally, discrepancies will occur in a team's responses to items. In Diana's assessment, the team acknowledged the possibility that behavior may be resulting in some delay or avoidance of nonpreferred activities, yet they did not suggest an escape-related replacement behavior, such as asking for a break, that would allow Diana a more appropriate way of delaying the transition. Any conflicting or ambiguous information should be noted and discussed with the team so that the information gathered leads the team to a better understanding of the purpose the challenging behavior serves. In addition, it is not uncommon for a behavior to have multiple functions. That is, a behavior can result in the student obtaining attention as well as producing escape from an undesirable circumstance. The goal of the PTR assessment is to help the team determine if the behavior serves different purposes under different environmental conditions, or if the behavior serves two functions simultaneously. If the behavior function changes contingent upon the conditions, separate hypotheses should be written. If the behavior serves two functions simultaneously, then the team should decide which function appears to serve as the major purpose. In this case, one hypothesis statement can be written.

Reinforce Component

A final scientific principle included in the PTR model is that behavior followed by desirable reinforcement tends to get stronger and is more likely to be repeated in the future under similar situations. Thus, the primary purpose of the Reinforce component is to identify consequences currently occurring after the challenging behavior that can be used to encourage desirable, prosocial behavior. It is imperative for the team to determine what is truly reinforcing for the student and to ensure that those reinforcers are provided when the desired, prosocial behavior is displayed—not when the challenging behavior is demonstrated. In particular, the team must identify the types (e.g., people, activities, items) and frequency of consequences that will help the student behave more appropriately by completing the Reinforce component of the FBA Checklist as accurately as possible.

In addition, accurate and complete information from this component will provide the team with support for or against the function they identified in the Teach component. In the Teach component in Figure 4.1, Diana's team indicated that Diana engaged in tantrum behavior to gain the teacher's attention. However, in the Reinforce component in Figure 4.3,

PTR FUNCTIONAL BEHAVIOR ASSESSMENT CHECKLIST

Problem behavior: __Tantrums__   Person responding: __Mrs. Jones (classroom teacher)__ Student: __Diana__

PTR Functional Behavior Assessment	TEACH Component

1. Does the *problem behavior* seem to be exhibited in order to **gain attention from peers**?

    ❏ Yes *(list the specific peers)* _____

    ☒ No

2. Does the *problem behavior* seem to be exhibited in order to **gain attention from adults**?
    If so, are there particular adults whose attention is solicited?

    ☒ Yes *(list the specific adults)* __Mrs. Jones (classroom teacher), Ms. Diaz (behavior specialist)__

    ❏ No

3. Does the *problem behavior* seem to be exhibited in order to **obtain objects** (e.g., toys or games, materials, food) from peers or adults?

    ❏ Yes *(list the specific objects)* _____

    ☒ No

4. Does the *problem behavior* seem to be exhibited in order to **delay a transition** from a preferred activity to a nonpreferred activity?

    ☒ Yes *(list the specific transition)* __Music, Art classes__

    ❏ No

5. Does the *problem behavior* seem to be exhibited in order to **terminate or delay** a nonpreferred (e.g., difficult, boring, repetitive) task or activity?

    ☒ Yes *(list the specific nonpreferred tasks or activities)* __Reading, Math__

    ❏ No

6. Does the *problem behavior* seem to be exhibited in order to **get away from** a nonpreferred classmate or adult?

    ❏ Yes *(list the specific peers or adults)* _____

    ☒ No

7. What **social skill(s)** could the student learn in order to reduce the likelihood of the *problem behavior* occurring in the future?

❏ Peer interaction	❏ Sharing objects	❏ Taking turns
❏ Play skills	❏ Sharing attention	❏ Losing gracefully
❏ Joint or shared attention	❏ Conversation skills	❏ Making prosocial statements
❏ Waiting for reinforcement	❏ Accepting differences	
☒ Getting attention appropriately		

    Other: _____

Figure 4.2. PTR Functional behavior assessment: Teach component.   *(continued)*

Figure 4.2. *(continued)*

8. What **problem-solving skill(s)** could the student learn in order to reduce the likelihood of the problem behavior occurring in the future?

❑ Recognizing need for help ❑ Note-taking strategies ❑ Staying engaged

❑ Asking for help ❑ Assignment management ❑ Working independently

❑ Ignoring peers ❑ Graphic organizers ❑ Working with a peer

❑ Making an outline ❑ Self-management

❑ Move ahead to easier items, then go back to difficult items

❑ Using visual supports to work independently

❑ Making choices from several appropriate options

Other: _____

9. What **communication skill(s)** could the student learn in order to reduce the likelihood of the problem behavior occurring in the future?

❑ Asking for a break ❑ Raising hand for attention ❑ Asking for help

❑ Requesting information ☒ Requesting wants ❑ Rejecting

❑ Active listening ❑ Commenting ❑ Responding to others

☒ Expressing emotions (frustration, anger, hurt)

Other: _____

Additional comments not addressed above in the **Teach component:** _____

_____

_____

_____

_____

they also noted that Diana was usually placed in time-out or sent to the behavior specialist's office after the tantrum behavior occurred, which minimized the amount of teacher attention she received. The team also identified that Diana was allowed to stay in a preferred class for a longer period of time (art and music), thus allowing her to escape or delay a nonpreferred activity (reading and math). Due to the conflicting information, the team reviewed their previously agreed-on function of obtaining teacher attention suggested in the Teach component. They then discussed the consequences that typically followed (e.g., removal from class, time-out or delay of upcoming activity) and most likely maintained (i.e., avoid/delay/escape) Diana's tantrum behavior. They agreed that the primary purpose of Diana's tantrum behavior may not be gaining the teacher's attention and decided that the team needed to revisit the questions on the Teach component of the assessment and consider an escape/avoid function as the primary purpose of challenging behavior. However, the information on the Reinforce section indicated that Diana enjoyed attention from the behavior specialist. The team concluded that while escape may be a primary motivator, a secondary function of Diana's challenging behavior might be to obtain time with and get attention from the behavior specialist.

COMPLETING THE PTR FUNCTIONAL BEHAVIOR ASSESSMENT CHECKLIST

The team should complete each PTR component (i.e., Prevent, Teach, Reinforce) of the FBA Checklist (see Appendix 4.1) for each challenging behavior targeted. When answering the questions on each checklist, the team should keep in mind the specific definition of the

Problem behavior: Tantrums   Person responding: Mrs. Jones (classroom teacher) Student: Diana

---

PTR Functional Behavior Assessment   **REINFORCE Component**

---

1. What **consequence(s)** usually follow the student's *problem behavior*?

    ☒ Sent to time-out   ☐ Gave personal space   ☐ Verbal reprimand

    ☐ Chair time-out   ☐ Stated rules   ☐ Head down

    ☐ Sent to office   ☐ Sent home   ☐ Calming/soothing

    ☐ Assistance given   ☐ Verbal redirect   ☒ Delay in activity

    ☐ Activity changed   ☐ Activity terminated   ☐ Physical prompt

    ☐ Peer reaction   ☐ Physical restraint   ☐ Removal of reinforcers

    ☒ Sent to behavior specialist/counselor

    ☐ Natural consequences (specify) _____

    Other: _Gets to stay in music and art a bit longer until she is ready to leave._

2. Does the student **enjoy praise** from teachers and other school staff? Does the student enjoy praise from some teachers more than others?

    ☒ Yes (*list specific people*) _Mrs. Jones (classroom teacher), Ms. Diaz (behavior specialist)_

    ☐ No

3. What is the likelihood of the student's **appropriate behavior** (e.g., on-task behavior, coopera-tion, successful performance) resulting in acknowledgment or praise from teachers or other school staff?

    ☐ Very likely   ☒ Sometimes   ☐ Seldom   ☐ Never

4. What is the likelihood of the student's **problem behavior** resulting in acknowledgment (e.g., reprimands, corrections) from teachers or other school staff?

    ☒ Very likely   ☐ Sometimes   ☐ Seldom   ☐ Never

5. What school-related items and activities are **most enjoyable** to the student? What items or activities could serve as special rewards?

    ☒ Social interaction with adults   ☒ Music   ☒ Art activity

    ☒ Social interaction with peers   ☐ Puzzles   ☒ Computer

    ☒ Playing a game   ☒ Going outside   ☐ Video games

    ☐ Helping teacher   ☐ Going for a walk ☐ Watching TV/video

    ☐ Extra PE time   ☐ Line leader   ☐ Reading

    ☐ Going to media center   ☐ Extra free time

    ☐ Sensory activity (specify) _____

    ☐ Food (specify)_____

    ☐ Objects (specify) _____

    Other: _____

Additional comments not addressed above in the **Reinforce component:** _____

_____

_____

_____

Figure 4.3.   PTR Functional behavior assessment: Reinforce component.

challenging behavior previously agreed on—not on other challenging behaviors that might be occurring in the classroom. The checklist should be completed by team members who have knowledge of the student and the challenging behavior. It is critical that team members contributing to the completion of the checklists have observed the student during the times and activities when the challenging behavior is most prevalent. All the relevant items should have responses and specific details provided as needed. It is more likely that effective interventions will be developed if the answers on the checklists are as specific, detailed, and inclusive as possible. The three assessment checklists should be completed in the order they are presented: 1) Prevent, 2) Teach, and 3) Reinforce.

COMPLETING THE PTR FUNCTIONAL BEHAVIOR ASSESSMENT SUMMARY TABLE

TIP   *Organizing PTR assessment information into patterns allows the team to accurately identify events in the environment that are related to the occurrence of the challenging behavior.*

Once the team has completed the FBA checklists, they should compile their responses using the FBA Summary Table (see Appendix 4.2). The FBA Summary Table will assist the team in developing final hypotheses, which will guide them toward selecting the most effective interventions. When summarizing the assessment information, it is important to identify patterns in the behavior. This will help the team to recognize events or circumstances that trigger and maintain challenging behavior, as well as those situations that are likely to result in desired prosocial behavior.

The FBA Summary Table is broken down into three columns that correspond to the three components of the FBA: Prevent data, Teach data, and Reinforce data. When summarizing the assessment information, responses should be listed under each relevant component. The team should begin by organizing the responses into patterns observed, rather than simply listing each answer. Organizing the data into patterns increases the likelihood that the team will develop an accurate hypothesis and begin to identify the most important circumstances for which intervention strategies should be developed.

Patterns can be established by organizing the data into categories under each component. For example, in Figure 4.4, prevention responses are organized by subject areas identified on the PTR Assessment as situations in which challenging behavior was likely to occur. The subject areas are further subdivided into the specific circumstances that set the stage for challenging behavior. Teach data are organized by major functions suggested by the team. Finally, Reinforce data are organized to show the connection between the team's hypothesized function suggested by the Teach data and the actual consequences that typically follow the student's challenging behavior. After grouping responses into categories or patterns, the team should review the FBA Summary Table and come to a consensus on the events that most likely trigger challenging behavior, the function of the challenging behavior (i.e., the reason or events that are most likely maintaining the challenging behavior), and the replacement behavior to be taught.

Diana's team developed the FBA Summary Table in Figure 4.5. During their discussion, team members noticed that challenging behavior occurred during the following times: 1) independent activities, 2) group activities, and 3) reading and math classes. However, it did not occur during science class, which included both independent and group activities. The teacher noted that Diana did well in reading and math classes despite challenging behavior. Once she got started, Diana was engaged and completed her work. The team then discussed the patterns of Diana's tantrum behavior further, specifically, the likelihood of tantrum

Behavior	PREVENT data	TEACH data	REINFORCE data

Tantrum (yell, scream, throw objects, hit)	Reading, math
	  Independent activities
	  Group activities
	Seat work
	Transitions from preferred activity
	  End of recess, art, music
	Told "no"
		To escape, delay, or avoid
		
		To obtain attention from the behavior specialist
			Sent to time-out
			Allowed to stay in art and music class
			Delay in upcoming activities
			
			Sent to behavior specialist

Prosocial behavior	Science
	  Independent activities
	  Group activities
	Recess, art, music
	When engaged in computer
		Communicating
		  Seeking attention
		  Asking for wants
		Transitioning appropriately
		Expressing emotions
			Enjoys time with behavior specialist
			Computer
			Recess, art, music

Figure 4.4. Organizing data to establish a pattern.

behavior occurring after art and music classes. Diana's teacher informed the team that classes were scheduled in the following order each day: art, reading, music, math, and science. The pattern that began to develop indicated that the end of the preferred activities (i.e., art and music) likely triggered the challenging behavior more than independent work activity did. Without analyzing the pattern of events that did and did not trigger challenging behavior, the team may have assumed that reading and math classes triggered Diana's tantrum behavior, rather than the end of the preferred activity, which would have made the intervention less likely to be effective.

TIP   *Stick to observable facts when identifying the function of the behavior. If team members talk about intentions or personality traits, ask what they have observed about the student to support these ideas.*

When reviewing the FBA Summary Table, it is important for the team to focus on facts rather than discuss opinions. For example, a team member might say, "Diana throws her pencil just to push my buttons." It is important to identify what has been directly observed that supports that opinion rather than relying on the comment alone. If a team member instead says, "When Diana throws her pencil in class, she looks to see if I'm watching," that member is relying on observable circumstances rather than opinion. Focusing on observable circumstances allows for identification of effective intervention strategies.

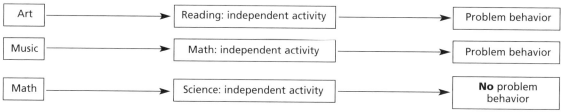

Figure 4.5. A graphic representation of a functional behavior assessment summary for Diana.

DEVELOPING THE HYPOTHESIS

Once the FBA Summary Table has been completed and the team has come to consensus on the information, the team should develop a hypothesis statement. This statement identifies why the challenging behavior is occurring (i.e., its function or purpose). Research has identified two basic functions of behavior:

1. *To get/obtain:* for example, to obtain attention from others (adults or peers), a preferred object or item, or access to a desired activity

2. *To escape/avoid:* for example, to escape a nonpreferred individual (adult or peer); escape or delay an undesirable activity, task, or situation (e.g., too noisy, chaotic or crowded; disagreeable smell, temperature, or light); or escape an undesirable social situation

An effective hypothesis statement should include information in three areas:

1. Antecedents or setting events that occur prior to the challenging behaviors (i.e., **when** the challenging behaviors occur)

2. Specific challenging behaviors demonstrated by the student as defined during the goal-setting process (e.g., **then** the student screams, hits, and throws objects)

3. Function or purpose of the behavior (e.g., **as a result,** the student escapes/avoids the math assignment; the student obtains or gets adult and peer attention)

For Diana, the team developed the following hypothesis statement based on the information obtained from the FBA Summary Table:

> When Diana is required to end art or music classes and begin independent work activities in reading and math classes, she will yell, scream, throw objects, and/or hit (i.e., tantrums). As a result, she is allowed to 1) delay or escape the independent work activities when she is sent to time-out or to the behavior specialist or allowed to stay in art or music classes and 2) get attention from the behavior specialist.

All the information in the hypothesis comes from the data on the FBA Summary Table. Specifically, information in the Prevent component (e.g., setting events and antecedents) of the FBA Summary Table includes the circumstances that are present or occur prior to the occurrence of challenging behavior. This data becomes the **when** portion of the hypothesis and assists the team with identifying the environmental events that can be changed to prevent challenging behavior from occurring. The **then** component in the second part of the hypothesis refers to the operational definition of the targeted challenging behavior(s) being assessed in the FBA. Finally, the information from the Teach component (i.e., function, purpose) of the FBA Summary Table, along with information from the Reinforce component that supports the hypothesized function, will be listed in the **as a result** component in the hypothesis. These data identify the function(s) of the challenging behavior and allow the team to identify alternative replacement behaviors to teach the student, which will serve the same function as the challenging behavior(s).

If the team has difficulty determining the hypothesis or gaining consensus on the function of the behavior, the following questions may assist them toward reaching that goal:

• Does the challenging behavior always occur under similar environmental conditions?

• Do the same behavior patterns occur in different environmental settings?

• Does the challenging behavior occur fairly equally across all environmental conditions?

• Does something happen immediately before the challenging behavior occurs or does the behavior occur after a time delay?

- Does the student have access to something after engaging in the challenging behavior that he or she did not have access to before?

- Was the student able to escape or delay something after engaging in the challenging behavior?

- Does the challenging behavior occur after the removal of a preferred item, activity, or individual?

- Does the challenging behavior occur with the presentation of a nonpreferred item, activity, or individual?

- What immediately follows the occurrence of the challenging behavior?

- What usually follows the display of appropriate behavior?

- Is more information needed? If so, what is the best way to obtain that information?

- Is an additional classroom observation needed? If so, when would be the best time to complete the observation based on occurrence and nonoccurrence of the targeted challenging behavior?

- Are other data collection measures needed in conjunction with the Behavior Rating Scale (see Chapter 3)? If so, which ones (e.g., frequency, latency, intensity, duration)?

- Would a brief interview with the parent or caregiver provide pertinent information?

In addition to developing a hypothesis for the challenging behavior, the team should develop a hypothesis for the specific replacement behavior or new skill that will be targeted during intervention using data from the FBA Summary Table. Developing this hypothesis is helpful in linking the function of challenging behavior to effective intervention strategies. Specifically, it is important that the replacement behavior matches the function of the challenging behavior and results in the same outcome as did the challenging behavior, to increase the likelihood that the student will use the new skill. Figure 4.6 provides hypotheses examples for Diana. The replacement behavior for Diana (i.e., asking for a break) should result in the same outcome as her challenging behavior (i.e., delaying the end of art and music classes, and the start of reading and math classes; getting attention from

	When	**Then**	**As a result**
Problem behavior	When Diana is required to end art or music and begin independent work activities in reading and math	Then, she will yell, scream, throw objects and/or hit (tantrum)	As a result, she is allowed to 1) delay or escape the independent work activities when she is sent to time-out or to the behavior specialist's office or allowed to stay in art and music classes, and 2) obtain attention from the behavior specialist.
Replacement behavior	When Diana is required to end art or music and begin independent work activities in reading and math	Then, she will ask for a break	As a result, she is allowed to delay or escape the independent work activities or allowed to stay in art or music, or obtains attention from the behavior specialist.

Figure 4.6.   Hypothesis statements based on the information obtained from the PTR Functional Behavior Assessment Summary Table (see Appendix 4.2) for Diana.

the behavior specialist). Developing a hypothesis for the replacement behavior assists the team in selecting function-based interventions.

TIP

The hypothesis is the essential link between the FBA and the behavior intervention plan. The components of the hypothesis must match the components of the intervention plan.

SUMMARY

By completing the FBA Checklist, the team should be able to identify environmental events that increase the likelihood of challenging behavior occurring. Organizing the information into patterns and developing a hypothesis that accurately reflects the environmental events related to the challenging behavior should allow the team to more accurately understand the conditions under which challenging behavior is likely to occur, as well as the intervention strategies that will effectively decrease challenging behavior and increase appropriate behavior. The hypothesis is the essential link between FBA and development of effective PTR interventions (see Chapter 5).

Appendix 4

Problem behavior: _____ Person responding: _____ Student: _____

Appendix 4.1.

PTR Functional Behavior Assessment Checklist

Directions:

1. The following Prevent-Teach-Reinforce (PTR) functional behavioral assessment (FBA) has three sections—Prevent, Teach, and Reinforce—and is 6 pages in length.

2. Complete one FBA for each problem behavior targeted on the behavior rating scale (BRS). For example, if both *hitting others* and *screaming* are listed on the BRS, two FBAs will be completed.

3. Do not complete the assessment on any prosocial/desired behaviors targeted on the BRS.

4. List the problem behavior on the top of each assessment form to ensure responses are given for that behavior only.

5. Answer each question by checking all the appropriate areas that apply, or by writing the response(s) that best describe events related to the problem behavior specified.

PTR Functional Behavior Assessment	**PREVENT Component**

1a. Are there *times of the school day* when problem behavior is *most likely* to occur? If yes, what are they?

❏ Morning ❏ Before meals ❏ During meals ❏ After meals ❏ Arrival

❏ Afternoon ❏ Dismissal Other:_____

1b. Are there *times of the school day* when problem behavior is *least likely* to occur? If yes, what are they?

❏ Morning ❏ Before meals ❏ During meals ❏ After meals ❏ Arrival

❏ Afternoon ❏ Dismissal Other:_____

2a. Are there *specific activities* when problem behavior is *very likely* to occur? If yes, what are they?

❏ Reading/LA ❏ Writing ❏ Math ❏ Science

❏ Independent work ❏ Small-group work ❏ Large-group work ❏ Riding the bus

❏ One-on-one ❏ Computer ❏ Recess ❏ Lunch

❏ Free time ❏ Peer/cooperative work ❏ Centers ❏ Discussions/Q&A

❏ Worksheets, seatwork ❏ Specials (specify) _____ ❏ Transitions (specify) _____

Other: _____

2b. Are there *specific activities* when cooperative and prosocial behavior is *very likely* to occur? What are they?

❏ Reading/LA ❏ Writing ❏ Math ❏ Science

❏ Independent work ❏ Small-group work ❏ Large-group work ❏ Riding the bus

❏ One-on-one ❏ Computer ❏ Recess ❏ Lunch

❏ Free time ❏ Peer/cooperative work ❏ Centers ❏ Discussions/Q&A

❏ Worksheets, seatwork ❏ Specials (specify) _____ ❏ Transitions (specify) _____

Other: _____

Prevent component (continued)

3a. Are there **specific classmates or adults** whose proximity is associated with a high likelihood of problem behavior? If so, who are they?

❏ Peers (specify) _____   ❏ Bus driver

❏ Teacher(s) (specify) _____   ❏ Parent

❏ Paraprofessional(s) (specify) _____

❏ Other school staff (specify) _____

❏ Other family member (specify) _____

Other: _____

3b. Are there **specific classmates or adults** whose proximity is associated with a high likelihood of cooperative and prosocial behavior? If so, who are they?

❏ Peers (specify) _____   ❏ Bus driver

❏ Teacher(s) (specify) _____   ❏ Parent

❏ Paraprofessional(s) (specify) _____

❏ Other school staff (specify) _____

❏ Other family member (specify) _____

Other: _____

4. Are there **specific circumstances** that are associated with a high likelihood of problem behavior?

❏ Request to start task   ❏ Task too difficult   ❏ Transition

❏ Being told work is wrong   ❏ Task too long   ❏ Student is alone

❏ Reprimand or correction   ❏ End of preferred activity   ❏ Unstructured time

❏ Told "no"   ❏ Task is boring   ❏ Novel task

❏ Seated near specific peer   ❏ Peer teasing or comments   ❏ Change in schedule

❏ Task is repetitive (same task daily)   ❏ Removal of preferred item

❏ Start of nonpreferred activity   ❏ Down time (no task specified)

❏ Teacher is attending to other students

Other: _____

5. Are there conditions in the **physical environment** that are associated with a high likelihood of problem behavior? For example, too warm or too cold, too crowded, too much noise, too chaotic, weather conditions....

❏ Yes (specify) _____

❏ No

6. Are there circumstances **unrelated to the school setting** that occur on some days and not other days that may make problem behavior more likely?

❏ Illness   ❏ No medication   ❏ Drug/alcohol abuse

❏ Allergies   ❏ Change in medication   ❏ Bus conflict

❏ Physical condition   ❏ Home conflict   ❏ Sleep deprivation

❏ Hunger   ❏ Fatigue   ❏ Parties or social event

❏ Change in diet   ❏ Change in routine   ❏ Parent not home

Problem behavior: _____ Person responding: _____ Student: _____

Prevent component (continued)

☐ Hormones or menstrual cycle

☐ Stayed with noncustodial parent

Other: _____

Additional comments not addressed above in the **Prevent component:** _____

_____

_____

_____

PTR Functional Behavior Assessment	**TEACH Component**

1. Does the *problem behavior* seem to be exhibited in order to **gain attention from peers**?

   ☐ Yes *(list the specific peers)* _____

   ☐ No

2. Does the *problem behavior* seem to be exhibited in order to **gain attention from adults**? If so, are there particular adults whose attention is solicited?

   ☐ Yes *(list the specific adults)* _____

   ☐ No

3. Does the *problem behavior* seem to be exhibited in order to **obtain objects** (e.g., toys or games, materials, food) from peers or adults?

   ☐ Yes *(list the specific objects)* _____

   ☐ No

4. Does the *problem behavior* seem to be exhibited in order to **delay a transition** from a preferred activity to a nonpreferred activity?

   ☐ Yes *(list the specific transition)* _____

   ☐ No

5. Does the *problem behavior* seem to be exhibited in order to **terminate or delay** a nonpreferred (e.g., difficult, boring, repetitive) task or activity?

   ☐ Yes *(list the specific nonpreferred tasks or activities)* _____

   ☐ No

6. Does the *problem behavior* seem to be exhibited in order to **get away from** a nonpreferred classmate or adult?

   ☐ Yes *(list the specific peers or adults)* _____

   ☐ No

Teach component (continued)

7. What *social skill(s)* could the student learn in order to reduce the likelihood of the *problem behavior* occurring in the future?

   ❏ Peer interaction ❏ Sharing objects ❏ Taking turns

   ❏ Play skills ❏ Sharing attention ❏ Losing gracefully

   ❏ Joint or shared attention ❏ Conversation skills ❏ Making prosocial statements

   ❏ Waiting for reinforcement ❏ Accepting differences

   ❏ Getting attention appropriately

   Other: _____

8. What *problem-solving skill(s)* could the student learn in order to reduce the likelihood of the problem behavior occurring in the future?

   ❏ Recognizing need for help ❏ Note-taking strategies ❏ Staying engaged

   ❏ Asking for help ❏ Assignment management ❏ Working independently

   ❏ Ignoring peers ❏ Graphic organizers ❏ Working with a peer

   ❏ Making an outline ❏ Self-management

   ❏ Move ahead to easier items, then go back to difficult items

   ❏ Using visual supports to work independently

   ❏ Making choices from several appropriate options

   Other: _____

9. What *communication skill(s)* could the student learn in order to reduce the likelihood of the problem behavior occurring in the future?

   ❏ Asking for a break ❏ Raising hand for attention ❏ Asking for help

   ❏ Requesting information ❏ Requesting wants ❏ Rejecting

   ❏ Active listening ❏ Commenting ❏ Responding to others

   ❏ Expressing emotions (frustration, anger, hurt)

   Other: _____

Additional comments not addressed above in the *Teach component:* _____

_____

_____

_____

Problem behavior: _____ Person responding: _____ Student: _____

PTR Functional Behavior Assessment	REINFORCE Component

1. What *consequence(s)* usually follow the student's *problem behavior*?

   ❏ Sent to time-out ❏ Gave personal space ❏ Verbal reprimand

   ❏ Chair time-out ❏ Stated rules ❏ Head down

   ❏ Sent to office ❏ Sent home ❏ Calming/soothing

   ❏ Assistance given ❏ Verbal redirect ❏ Delay in activity

   ❏ Activity changed ❏ Activity terminated ❏ Physical prompt

   ❏ Peer reaction ❏ Physical restraint ❏ Removal of reinforcers

   ❏ Sent to behavior specialist/counselor

   ❏ Natural consequences (specify) _____

   Other: _____

2. Does the student *enjoy praise* from teachers and other school staff? Does the student enjoy praise from some teachers more than others?

   ❏ Yes (*list specific people*) _____

   ❏ No

3. What is the likelihood of the student's *appropriate behavior* (e.g., on-task behavior, cooperation, successful performance) resulting in acknowledgment or praise from teachers or other school staff?

   ❏ Very likely ❏ Sometimes ❏ Seldom ❏ Never

4. What is the likelihood of the student's *problem behavior* resulting in acknowledgment (e.g., reprimands, corrections) from teachers or other school staff?

   ❏ Very likely ❏ Sometimes ❏ Seldom ❏ Never

5. What school-related items and activities are *most enjoyable* to the student? What items or activities could serve as special rewards?

   ❏ Social interaction with adults ❏ Music ❏ Art activity

   ❏ Social interaction with peers ❏ Puzzles ❏ Computer

   ❏ Playing a game ❏ Going outside ❏ Video games

   ❏ Helping teacher ❏ Going for a walk ❏ Watching TV/video

   ❏ Extra PE time ❏ Line leader ❏ Reading

   ❏ Going to media center ❏ Extra free time

   ❏ Sensory activity (specify) _____

   ❏ Food (specify) _____

   ❏ Objects (specify) _____

   Other: _____

Prevent-Teach-Reinforce: The School-Based Model of Individualized Positive Behavior Support by G. Dunlap, R. Iovannone, D. Kincaid, K. Wilson, K. Christiansen, P. Strain, and C. English.

Reinforce component (continued)

Additional comments not addressed above in the ***Reinforce component:*** _____

_____

_____

_____

PTR Functional Behavior Assessment Summary Table

Directions:

1. Gather all Prevent-Teach-Reinforce (PTR) Functional Behavior Assessments (FBAs) completed for one problem behavior (see Appendix 4.1).

2. List the problem behavior on the FBA Summary Table.

3. Starting with one completed FBA, list events in the respective Prevent, Teach, and Reinforce columns, beginning to identify and group information in patterns.

4. Do the same for events marked for the prosocial behavior.

5. Continue grouping information into the current patterns (or new ones as needed) as the remaining completed FBAs are summarized.

6. As a team, identify the data in the Prevent section that are most likely to result in problem behavior *or* that are most likely to result in problem behavior that is most disruptive to the classroom. List the agreed-upon events in the *When* box of the possible hypothesis.

7. As a team, discuss any discrepancies in the teaching and reinforcement data to ensure an accurate function of problem behavior is identified. List the agreed-upon events in the *as a result* box of the possible hypothesis.

8. As a team, identify the broad category of behavior or the specific replacement behavior the student needs to be taught. List the agreed-upon behavior in the *replacement behavior* box of possible hypotheses.

Student _____   School _____   Date _____

Behavior	PREVENT data	TEACH data	REINFORCE data

Possible hypotheses

	When	Then	As a result
Problem behavior			
Replacement behavior			

Behavior Intervention Plan

5

OVERVIEW AND OBJECTIVES

After completion of the Prevent-Teach-Reinforce (PTR) functional behavior assessment and the development of a hypothesis, the next step in the PTR model is to develop an individualized behavior intervention plan. The PTR Behavior Intervention Plan includes a minimum of three components:

1. A Prevent intervention

2. A Teach intervention

3. A Reinforce intervention

Each intervention strategy selected must match the results from the PTR functional behavior assessment and be able to be implemented in the student's classroom.

Chapter 5 focuses on the following objectives:

- Identifying at least one Prevent, one Teach, and one Reinforce intervention

- Developing a step-by-step plan to implement the interventions

- Developing a plan for training and technical assistance

- Developing a measure of fidelity of implementation

In achieving the objectives of this chapter, the following forms may be helpful: PTR Intervention Checklist, PTR Intervention Scoring Table, PTR Behavior Intervention Plan, PTR Behavior Intervention Plan (alternate version), PTR Training Checklist, and PTR Fidelity of Implementation (see Appendixes 5.1–5.6, respectively). Blank copies of these forms are also included on the accompanying CD-ROM.

COMPONENTS OF THE BEHAVIOR INTERVENTION PLAN

To develop an effective intervention plan, team members should refer to the hypotheses developed for the challenging behavior and the replacement behavior identified during the functional behavior assessment process in Chapter 4. Each component of the hypothesis will assist the team in selecting the appropriate interventions for the student by allowing them to match the function of the challenging behavior and conditions under which it occurs with strategies that are most likely to be effective in preventing challenging behavior and increasing appropriate behavior. It is very important that the team select at least one Prevent, one Teach, and one Reinforce intervention for the PTR Behavior Intervention Plan.

TIP

Many teams have found that Prevent strategies are easier to implement than Teach or Reinforce strategies, but all three are essential elements of an intervention plan.

Prevent Interventions

Before selecting Prevent interventions, the team should review the Prevent data and the *when* component of the hypothesis in the PTR Functional Behavior Assessment Summary Table (see Chapter 4). This information identifies the environmental circumstances associated with a high likelihood of challenging behavior. Prevent strategies serve to change these situations, thus making the student's challenging behavior unnecessary or irrelevant.

For example, Rachel was most likely to engage in challenging behavior during writing assignments that required using appropriate capitalization and writing the upper case letters so that the top of the letters touched the upper line on the paper. While reviewing the prevention interventions, the team decided to use the Curricular Modification strategy. They agreed to adapt Rachel's writing paper by coloring the top lines of the writing paper and the letters to be capitalized red. These modifications were designed to assist Rachel in determining which letters should be capitalized and to make it easier to meet the requirement of having the top of the letter touch the top of the line. This Prevent strategy eliminated the trigger for challenging behavior (i.e., not knowing which letters should be capitalized and should touch the top line), thus making the challenging behavior unnecessary and less likely to occur.

In addition, Prevent data also indicate when a student is most likely to engage in appropriate or prosocial behavior. These data can assist the team in determining what environmental circumstances already are in place that predict the occurrence of appropriate behavior. When reviewing the PTR Functional Behavior Assessment Summary Table for the occurrence of appropriate prosocial behavior, the team might ask the following questions to help identify effective intervention strategies:

1. How can these events and/or circumstances be increased within the environment?

2. How can these situations be replicated during those times when challenging behavior is most likely to occur?

The best time to teach a new behavior is when the student is not engaging in challenging behavior. Thus, it is critical to implement Prevent strategies that will decrease the likelihood that challenging behavior will occur.

TIP

It is tempting for teams to "overshoot" on replacement behaviors by requiring the student to engage in complex behaviors to achieve a desired outcome. Keeping the replacement behavior simple and one that is in the student's repertoire is key.

Teach Interventions

As the team begins to select Teach interventions, they should first review the Teach data and the *will* component of the hypothesis in the PTR Functional Behavior Assessment Summary Table (see Chapter 4). This information identifies the function (purpose) of the challenging behavior and allows the team to identify alternative behaviors that will be more effective as a replacement. The replacement behavior can be one of two types, both of which can be effective as desirable substitutes for existing challenging behavior. The first type is a behavior that is *functionally equivalent* to the challenging behavior. This means that the replacement behavior leads to the same reinforcer or outcome as the challenging behavior. Another way of saying this is to say that the replacement behavior and the challenging behavior are in the same "response class" (Carr, 1988). For example, when given an independent writing assignment, Rachel would leave her seat and wander around the room. The functional behavior assessment identified the reinforcer (desired outcome) of this behavior as escape from the nonpreferred writing assignment. In this instance, a functionally equivalent replacement behavior would be for Rachel to raise her hand and ask for a break. This would be considered functionally equivalent because the reinforcer is the same as the challenging behavior—that is, escape from the writing assignment.

The second type of replacement behavior is behavior that is *physically incompatible* with the challenging behavior. For instance, for Rachel, remaining in her seat and continuing to work on her writing assignment is both desirable and physically incompatible with leaving her seat and wandering around the classroom. The reinforcer for this incompatible behavior would be (presumably) attention and praise delivered by her teacher, though other more powerful reinforcers (such as stickers, tokens, or extra time at recess or other favored activity) could also be scheduled.

There are a number of considerations for a team to weigh in selecting a type of replacement behavior, as well as the specific behavior itself. Some of the considerations include 1) how urgent is the need for behavior change; 2) whether the replacement behavior is already in the student's repertoire or whether it would take time and effort to teach the behavior; 3) which behavior is most desirable and acceptable in the designated setting, such as the classroom; and 4) whether the reinforcers to be used in intervention can compete effectively with the reinforcers that are already maintaining the student's challenging behavior. One advantage of a functionally equivalent replacement behavior is that we already know that the reinforcer is effective. In Rachel's case, for example, the reinforcer for both the problem (leaving her seat and wandering around) and the replacement behavior (asking for a break) is temporary escape from the writing assignment, so it can be safely assumed that the reinforcer is effective. On the other hand, the functionally equivalent replacement behavior may not be ultimately satisfactory as a behavioral goal, and the team may prefer to move toward a goal of prolonged task engagement and task completion. Therefore, in Rachel's case, in addition to honoring a request for a break, the team might also temporarily modify the assignment so that it is easier and more appealing and gradually require a longer period of task engagement before providing the break. The team could also supplement the extended period of task engagement with additional attention and praise from the teacher, thus combining replacement behaviors.

TIP   *Remember that the potency of reinforcers can change over time. Be prepared to change consequences if the data so dictate.*

Reinforce Interventions

The team is now ready to select Reinforce interventions. They should first review the Reinforce data and *as a result* component of the hypothesis in the PTR Functional Behavior Assessment Summary Table (see Chapter 4). This information identifies why the student may continue to engage in challenging behavior and provides the team with data on how to make the student's challenging behavior ineffective. It is important for the team to change how adults and/or peers respond to the student's challenging behavior so that the student no longer gets a desired outcome (i.e., escape or obtain) for the inappropriate behavior.

It is important for the team to consider how their current methods of responding to the student's challenging behavior may unintentionally serve as reinforcement. Developing an alternate behavior and delivering the reinforcement or desired outcome contingent on the student engaging in the appropriate behavior is an important step in making the new skill effective. However, there will be times when the student will continue to engage in the challenging behavior, particularly if the challenging behavior has a long history of being effective for the student. The team should address strategies to be implemented that will follow inappropriate behavior (if it occurs) so that it is no longer an effective way for the student's behavior to be reinforced. The Reinforce data in the PTR Functional Behavior Assessment Summary Table from Chapter 4 can also identify additional items and activities that are reinforcing for the student. The team could use this information to provide extra (or bonus) reinforcers to increase the likelihood that the student will engage in the desired prosocial behavior.

For example, the team taught Rachel to ask for a break when she was presented with the writing task. When she engaged in this functionally equivalent replacement behavior, she was allowed to take a brief break during which she could move around the classroom quietly. However, the team really wanted Rachel to complete her work—the more desired, prosocial replacement behavior. Using information from the PTR Functional Behavior Assessment Summary Table, the team determined that in addition to escaping her work, Rachel enjoyed attention from the behavior specialist. Thus, the team taught Rachel that if she completed her assignment, she could go to the behavior specialist's office for 10 minutes during the next activity. Furthermore, the team decided that if Rachel did engage in challenging behavior, she would not be sent to the behavior specialist's office. Instead, the teacher would remind Rachel that she could ask for a break if she needed time away from her work and everyone in the room would continue working without talking to Rachel (i.e., challenging behavior would be placed on extinction).

The team used the Reinforce data to make both behaviors identified in the Teach component (escape/break from work and complete assignment) more effective than the challenging behavior at getting Rachel out of doing her work. However, by incorporating extra or bonus reinforcers into the plan, the team was able to increase the likelihood that Rachel would engage in the desired prosocial replacement behavior because she got out of doing work *and* received attention from the behavior specialist.

BEHAVIOR INTERVENTION OPTIONS FOR THE PTR COMPONENTS

This section provides a short description of each of the PTR intervention strategies. The team should keep in mind the information summarized on the PTR Functional Behavior Assessment Summary Table and the hypothesis developed by the team in Chapter 4. This information will assist with identifying the most effective strategies for the student's behavior intervention plan. For a summary listing of the interventions, readers may refer to Appendix 5.1.

Behavior Interventions for the Prevent Component

This section provides intervention descriptions that can prevent a student's challenging behavior from occurring and may be considered for use within the Prevent section of the behavior plan. For prevention strategies to be effective, they should involve the removal or alteration of the antecedent event that triggers the challenging behavior. The strategies selected by the team should alter or remove the events identified in the *when* section of the hypothesis. For an overview and examples of many of the following prevention strategies, see Kern and Clemens (2007).

Providing Choices

This intervention provides the student with a choice between two or more options. Choice making can be used to enhance the student's participation in an activity or task that typically results in challenging behavior when a direct demand is delivered.

Uses

Consider using this intervention when the PTR assessment information indicates that

- Challenging behavior occurs when demands are made of the student.
- Challenging behavior occurs when transitioning from preferred to nonpreferred activities.
- The student uses behavior to get control.

- The student uses behavior to protest situations.
- The student has minimal or no choice-making opportunities throughout the day.

Examples

Examples include the following:

- Choosing materials to use in a task (e.g., pen color)
- Choosing between different tasks (e.g., math versus writing)
- Choosing where to work (e.g., desk versus table)
- Choosing when to do a task (e.g., writing first, math second)
- Choosing a person to work with (e.g., Max or Sue)
- Choosing to end an activity (e.g., when to stop art and start journal)
- Refusing an option (e.g., decline a specific food item at snack time)

Considerations for Implementation

The team should ensure that the choices are indeed available and that all parties will support whatever choice is made.

Sample References

Sample references include Cole, Davenport, Bambara, and Ager (1997); Romaniuk et al. (2002); Shogren, Faggella-Luby, and Bae (2004); and Tiger, Hanley, and Hernandez (2006).

Transition Supports

This intervention provides the student with a cue or sequence of cues prior to a change. The change can be switching to a different activity, moving to a new location, or preparing the student for new people. Cues can be visual, auditory, motoric, or a combination. Presenting a cue prior to a transition allows the student to predict the sequence of events. Transition supports can be individualized (e.g., built into an individual schedule or only available to this student) or used for the entire class.

Uses

Consider using this intervention when the PTR hypothesis indicates that

- The student does not understand what is expected during a transition.
- The student has difficulty physically moving from one activity to another.
- The student has difficulty reengaging in the next activity or ending a preferred activity.

Examples

Examples include the following:

- Auditory (e.g., playing a song, chanting a phrase, providing an audible cue such as a bell or chimes)
- Visual (e.g., showing a symbol or picture, flipping over a sign, pointing out a visual timer)
- Motoric (e.g., having a dance or physical movement associated with upcoming changes in activities)

Considerations for Implementation

It is important to provide a consistent routine or ritual for transition supports. The routine cue will allow the student to quickly predict an upcoming change. The student may need direct instruction in the specific behaviors to perform while making the transition (e.g., lining up, walking in the hallways) and reinforcement for performing the appropriate behaviors.

Sample References

Sample references include Cote, Thompson, and McKerchar (2005); Sainato, Strain, Lefebvre, and Rapp (1987); Tustin (1995).

Environmental Supports

Environmental supports are visual and/or auditory symbols that let the student understand what is currently happening in the environment, what will be happening throughout the day, or scheduled changes in routines. The symbols can be objects, pictures, written words, or icons.

Uses

Consider using this intervention when the PTR assessment information indicates that challenging behavior occurs when

- The student has difficulty understanding what is happening within the environment.

- The student has difficulty with transitions from activity to activity, setting to setting, or person to person.

- The student has difficulty understanding options or choices.

- The student is required to end an activity or task.

- The student experiences a change in routine or schedule.

- The student does not understand expectations that are not clearly defined or established.

Examples

Examples include the following:

- Schedules (i.e., a visual sequence of the day's activities)

- Choice boards (i.e., a visual display of activities or reinforcers from which to choose)

- Boundary identification (e.g., providing a carpet square with the student's name to sit on, using a checkered tablecloth for snack time and a striped tablecloth for art time)

- Labels (i.e., placing photographs, pictures, or written word symbols on objects and areas)

- Activity ending (i.e., visual or auditory symbols indicating the end of an activity; e.g., having a finished folder to place daily activities as completed, visual or auditory timers)

Considerations for Implementation

Direct instruction is often required to teach the appropriate use of the specific support. In addition, the student's level of symbol understanding should be determined first. Some students will need concrete representation such as actual or miniature objects, whereas others will understand photographs, colored or black-and-white drawings, or written words. A speech pathologist may be able to assist with this determination.

Sample References

Sample references include Clarke, Dunlap, and Vaughn (1999); Dooley, Wilczenski, and Torem (2001); and Mesibov, Browder, and Kirkland (2002).

Curricular Modifications

Curricular modifications are changes in instructional tasks that lessen the likelihood of challenging behavior occurring on presentation to the student. There are two main categories of curricular modifications: change in the content of the instruction or change in the presentation of the task.

Uses

Consider using this intervention when the PTR assessment information indicates that

- Challenging behavior occurs when academic demands are made of the student.
- Challenging behavior occurs when the student is presented with a nonpreferred academic task.
- The student engages in challenging behavior to escape an academic demand.
- The student refuses to engage in an academic task.

Examples

Types of curricular modifications include presentation and content modification. In presentation modification, tasks are presented in a way that makes the activity less distasteful and increases the likelihood that the student will do the task. Examples include the following:

- Task alternation (e.g., novel to familiar, maintenance to acquisition, nonpreferred to preferred, teacher-directed to independent, lecture to interactive activities)
- Task division (i.e., break task up into smaller units)
- Providing choices
- Varying materials

For example, a mathematics worksheet with four rows of problems can be cut into four strips. The student can be given one strip at a time, making the worksheet less overwhelming. As the student completes each row, it can be turned in to be checked, providing an opportunity for reinforcement of appropriate work behaviors.

Examples

Content modification is when academic activities are modified to be more meaningful. Examples include the following:

- Task difficulty (e.g., adjust level of difficulty, provide errorless learning opportunities, teach replacement skills, shorten task and then gradually increase length or time)
- Task preference (i.e., incorporate the student's interests)
- Task meaningfulness (i.e., make task functional and relevant to the student)

For example, rather than doing a sorting activity on a worksheet, the student could sort chocolate and white milk cartons in the cafeteria before lunch begins.

Considerations for Implementation

The team should make sure that the student has the skills to do the curricular requirements. Additionally, they should think about ways to make the activity more motivating and interesting. Incorporating the student's preferred interests into an activity can result in the student participating without challenging behavior.

Sample References

Sample references include Armendariz and Umbreit (1999); Cooper et al. (1992); Iovannone & Dunlap (2001); Kern, Delaney, Clarke, Dunlap, and Childs (2001); Lambert, Cartledge, and Heward (2006); Moore, Anderson, and Kumar (2005); Vaughn and Horner (1997).

Adult Verbal Behavior

In this intervention, the teacher provides frequent positive attention to the student. This allows the student to associate the teacher (and instructional demands) with positive feelings and allows for attention without the student displaying a challenging behavior.

Uses

Consider using this intervention when PTR Assessment information indicates:

- The student does not have a positive relationship with adults.

- The student enjoys attention and praise from adults.

- The student gets more acknowledgment from the adults when performing challenging behavior and less acknowledgment when performing appropriate behavior.

Examples

Examples include the following:

- Giving positive statements to the student at a high ratio

- Keeping an even tone and volume

- Using positive language, even when redirecting

- Using clear, specific language when asking the student to do an activity

- Making more comments than demands when working with the student

For example, the demand "You need to work much faster" may trigger challenging behavior, whereas making a comment such as "You are trying so hard to finish" may prompt the student to work harder.

Considerations for Implementation

Attempt to keep a 4:1 ratio of positive to negative statements. To assist in meeting this ratio, a teacher might put smiley faces around the room. Each time the teacher sees a smiley face, it will prompt him or her to make a positive statement. Another way is to set a daily goal of the number of positive statements to be made. The same number of paper clips could be put in the teacher's right pocket. Each time the teacher makes a positive statement, a paper clip can be moved from the right pocket to the left one.

Sample References

Sample references include Allday and Pakurar (2007), and Matheson and Shriver (2005).

Classroom Management

This intervention involves setting up a clear, comprehensible system of how a classroom will operate and how daily activities will occur so that appropriate behavior is encouraged and rewarded. When classrooms have clear rules for appropriate behavior that are consistently taught and reinforced, teachers spend less time addressing challenging behaviors.

Uses

Consider using this intervention when the PTR assessment information indicates

- The student does not understand classroom behavioral expectations.

- The student does not possess the needed skills to behave appropriately in the classroom.

- Challenging behavior arises when classroom management is enforced in a negative manner.

- There is a need for more clear and consistent behavioral expectations.

Examples

Examples include the following:

- Arranging the classroom environment for easy access to students, and so students can move without disturbing peers

- Providing opportunities for the student to show appropriate rule-following behavior

- Prompting the student for appropriate behavior before the chance to exhibit inappropriate behavior

- Embedding classroom rules into daily lessons and activities

A specific behavior can be the focus each week. For example, the rule of *speak kindly to others* can be a theme for instructional activities. The student (along with the rest of the class) can play detective and count how many times the student, and others, are "caught in the act" of speaking kindly.

Considerations for Implementation

Effective classroom management strategies promote appropriate behavior for all students, not just the student with challenging behavior. Often, students do not understand classroom expectations or may not have the skills to behave appropriately. By consistently teaching rules and providing opportunities for practice, the student will acquire, maintain, and generalize the skills.

Sample References

Sample references include Colvin, Sugai, and Patching (1993); Darch and Kameenui (2003); Jones and Jones (2001); Lohrmann and Talerico (2004).

Increased Noncontingent Reinforcement

In this intervention, the teacher responds positively to the student independent of the occurrence of a desired prosocial or replacement behavior, which may include providing attention, access to desired activities, or escape from tasks. The response delivered should be reinforcing to the student; it may or may not be based on the function of the challenging behavior. Delivery of noncontingent reinforcement should occur as long as the student is not engaging in an inappropriate behavior, even if the student is simply sitting in a chair, standing in line, or raising a hand.

Uses

Consider using this intervention when the PTR hypothesis indicates that

- The student responds positively to praise or acknowledgment from the teacher.

- The student seeks to gain teacher or adult attention.

- The student enjoys the attention of certain peers.

- The student exhibits interest in specific classroom activities or school-related items.

Examples

Examples include when the teacher provides the student with a high degree of attention (a reinforcer for the student) during situations in which the challenging behavior typically occurs, thus preventing the need for the student to perform the undesired behavior.

Considerations for Implementation

It often is useful to set a time schedule for positively interacting with the student. The time schedule should be individualized to the needs of the student and should be based on the frequency of challenging behavior exhibited, especially if the challenging behavior is used to gain access to attention. Over time, the schedule is lengthened and may become varied rather than a set time schedule. Delivery of the reinforcer should occur as long as the student is not engaging in an inappropriate behavior. Exactly what the student is doing is not important, as long as it is appropriate.

Sample References

Sample references include Carr et al. (2000); Jones, Drew, and Weber (2000); and Rasmussen and O'Neill (2006).

Setting Event Modifications

In this intervention, the teacher alters conditions in the student's environment when setting events are present. *Setting events* are environmental conditions or patterns that set off the student's behavior but are removed in time from the behavior's occurrence. The setting event can happen from a few minutes to a few hours before the behavior, such as missing the bus, arriving late, having a fight with a sibling, or staying with a noncustodial parent. Although the event does not occur immediately before the challenging behavior, it sets the stage for the behavior to happen later or throughout the day.

Uses

Consider using this intervention when the PTR Assessment information indicates that

- Challenging behaviors are influenced by the student's proximity to or interactions with individuals such as peers, teachers, school staff, or family members.

- Challenging behaviors occur during a specific school activity, class, or event.

- Challenging behaviors occur during a specific time in the school day.
- Challenging behaviors occur whenever there is a change in the student's out-of-school routine, schedule, or lifestyle (e.g., missing the bus or arriving late to school; holiday breaks, weekends, or absences; lack of sleep; lack of necessary or appropriate clothing; rotating between family member households; missing meals or medication).

Examples

Examples include the following:

- Providing a flexible schedule that allows the student to start the day with preferred tasks and to settle down, which works well when the setting event occurs before school
- Providing a safe area for the student to talk about feelings or events, or get assistance with a task that is less likely to be done when a setting event is present
- Presenting a series of requests the student will comply with before asking the student to do an activity that typically results in challenging behavior (e.g., deliver three to five short requests that the student will do before delivering the one that the student usually does not do)
- Setting up a check-in time when students can identify how they are feeling and access help to calm themselves, if necessary

Considerations for Implementation

Because many setting events may occur in the student's home environment, good communication with the student's caregiver is essential.

Sample References

Sample references include Kennedy and Itkonen (1993); McLaughlin and Carr (2005); and Shores, Gunter, and Jack (1993).

Opportunities for Prosocial Behavior (Peer Support)

This intervention involves providing peers with skills to elicit appropriate social behavior from the student and providing reinforcement on the occurrence of the behavior. Peer supports can be provided in several ways, including cooperative working, tutoring, or peer buddies.

Uses

Consider using this intervention when the PTR assessment information indicates that

- Challenging behavior results in peer attention.
- Peer relationships are limited and of low quality.

Examples

Examples include the following:

- Arrange for the student to work with a peer or a group of peers in a cooperative activity. Group arrangement should consider the skills each peer has so everyone has a chance for meaningful input.

- Assign specific peer tutors to work with the student. Peer tutors should be liked by the child and should not be in charge of redirecting or reprimanding the student. Peer tutors should be taught strategies to use when working on an academic task with the student.

- Train a group of three to five peers in strategies that will enable them to elicit and encourage prosocial behavior from the focus student.

Considerations for Implementation

Careful selection of peers is critical when implementing this strategy, along with specific training in strategies to be used. Peer groups are most successful when adults provide coaching and feedback to the peers during the orientation on the use of the strategy. Adults can fade their presence as the peers become more skilled in supporting the student. The teacher should meet with the peers regularly to debrief situations and determine future activities.

Sample References

Sample references include Cushing and Kennedy (1997); Gillies and Ashman (1997); Strain, Schwartz, & Bovey (2008), Sutherland and Snyder (2007); and Telecsan, Slaton, and Stevens (1999).

Peer Modeling or Peer Reinforcement

This intervention involves the acknowledgment of and rewarding of peers who engage in appropriate behavior as a model for how a student should behave.

Uses

Consider using this intervention when the PTR assessment information indicates that

- The likelihood of the student engaging in prosocial behavior increases when he or she is in close proximity to specific peers.

- Challenging behavior is associated with the student's proximity to, or interactions with, certain peers.

- Challenging behavior is likely to occur during specific activities or during certain times of the day.

Example

If the desired behavior of the student with challenging behavior is to raise his or her hand, the teacher will recognize another student who raises his or her hand to ask a question, by saying, "Thank you for raising your hand when you had a question. You earned a surprise at the end of the day."

Considerations for Implementation

This strategy may not be effective with some students with disabilities. It is important that the student is able to and does attend to such cues in the classroom for this strategy to be effective. The strategy is relatively easy to use as long as there are other students in the classroom who reliably engage in the targeted behavior.

Sample References

Sample references include Jones, Young, and Friman (2000); Schunk (1987); and Werts, Caldwell, and Wolery (1996).

Interventions for the Teach Component

This section describes interventions for new behaviors that may be considered within the Teach section of the behavior plan. On the PTR Intervention Checklist (see Figure 5.1 and Appendix 5.1), note that the Teach strategy titled Replacement Behavior is marked with a double asterisk (**). It is essential that each PTR Behavior Intervention Plan include at least one new skill or appropriate behavior to be taught that is linked to the functional behavior assessment information. Research suggests that function-based intervention plans are more effective than those that are not function based (Ingram, Lewis-Palmer, & Sugai, 2005; Newcomer & Lewis, 2004). For strategies to be effective, they should teach the student a new skill that will serve the same purpose (i.e., result in the same outcome) as the challenging behavior. Therefore, it will be useful for the team to review the hypotheses of challenging behavior and desired behavior developed in Chapter 4 before selecting from the following strategies. This will ensure that the strategies selected by the team will teach the student a skill that will serve the same purpose as the challenging behavior.

Replacement Behaviors (Functionally Equivalent)

In this intervention, appropriate alternative behaviors that result in the student getting the same outcome as the challenging behavior are taught.

Hypothesis: ***When*** Rachel is given an independent writing assignment, she ***will*** get out of her seat, wander around the room, and talk to peers until the teacher sends her to the behavior specialist. ***As a result,*** she is able to **escape** her work and **obtain attention from the behavior specialist**.

PREVENT Interventions	TEACH Interventions	REINFORCE Interventions
	**Replacement Behavior	****Reinforce Replacement Behavior**
_1_ Providing choices	_1_ Functionally equivalent	_2_ Functionally equivalent
__ Transition supports	__ Physically incompatible	__ Physically incompatible
_3_ Environmental supports	__ Specific academic skills	_1_ Discontinue Reinforcement of Problem Behavior
_2_ Curricular modification (eliminating triggers)	_2_ Problem-solving strategies	_3_ Group contingencies (peer, teacher)
__ Adult verbal behavior (just be nice)	__ General coping strategies	__ Increase ratio of + to − responses
__ Classroom management	__ Specific social skills	__ Home-to-school reinforcement system
__ Increase noncontingent reinforcement	__ Teacher-pleasing behaviors	__ Delayed gratification
__ Setting event modification	__ Learning skills strategies	
__ Opportunity for prosocial behavior (peer support)	_3_ Self-management (self-monitoring)	
__ Peer modeling or peer reinforcement	__ Independent responding	
	__ Increased engaged time	

Does the severity or intensity of the student's problem behavior pose a threat to self or others? ❏ Yes ❏ No
If yes, is a crisis intervention plan needed?   ❏ Yes   ❏ No

Figure 5.1. Rachel's PTR Intervention Checklist (see Appendix 5.1).

Uses

Consider using this intervention when the PTR assessment information indicates that

- Challenging behavior is used to escape, avoid, or delay a nonpreferred task, undesired activity, or a specific adult or peer.
- Challenging behavior is used to gain attention from adults or peers.
- Challenging behavior is used to obtain a concrete object or gain access to an activity.
- Challenging behavior is used to delay transitions from preferred to nonpreferred activities.
- Challenging behavior is used to obtain control over a situation.

Examples

Examples include the following:

- Asking for assistance
- Requesting a break to briefly escape
- Requesting attention

Considerations for Implementation

When selecting functionally equivalent replacement behaviors, the replacement behavior should be more efficient and less effortful at getting the payoff than the challenging behavior. Ensure that the replacement behavior has an equivalent function or outcome as the challenging behavior. That is, if the student's behavior appears to be a way of escaping a task, the replacement behavior also should allow the student to escape the task. Choosing a replacement behavior that serves a different function (e.g., getting attention) will most likely be ineffective.

Sample References

Sample references include Dufrene, Doggett, and Henington (2007); and Reichle and Johnston (1993).

Replacement Behaviors (Physically Incompatible)

This intervention involves teaching and reinforcing replacement behaviors that are physically incompatible with, and more appropriate and socially desirable than, the challenging behavior.

Uses

Consider using this intervention when the PTR assessment information indicates that

- Challenging behavior is due to ineffective and/or inefficient communication or social skills.
- Skill deficits in pivotal behaviors prevent the student from accessing typical environments with typical peers or achieving short-term goals.

Examples

Examples include the following:

- Teaching the student a system so he or she will be able to continue to work on difficult tasks rather than engaging in an escape or avoidance behavior (e.g., circling items that the student is unsure of and moving on to familiar items)

- Teaching prosocial behaviors that allow the student to obtain reinforcers rather than engaging in an inappropriate attention-getting behavior (e.g., appropriately joining an activity or game in progress)

- Selecting, prompting, and reinforcing any desired behavior (social, academic, recreational) that cannot be performed at the same time as the targeted challenging behavior

Considerations for Implementation

When teaching desired or pro-social replacement behaviors, the teacher should provide reinforcement that is at least as powerful as the reinforcer that maintains the challenging behavior. An additional powerful and appropriate reinforcement may be delivered contingent on performance of the desired behavior that will provide increased motivation for the student to perform the desired behavior.

Sample References

Sample references include Halle, Bambara, and Reichle (2005) and Kern and Kokina (2008).

Specific Academic Skills

This intervention involves teaching a student basic skills (e.g., reading, writing, math) that will allow the student to be actively engaged and to complete instructional activities. This strategy is related to the previous strategy (physically incompatible replacement behaviors), but focuses on academic performance.

Uses

Consider using this intervention when the PTR assessment information indicates that

- Challenging behavior occurs during academic tasks that are difficult or novel

- The student may not have the requisite skills to perform the academic tasks

Examples

Examples include the following:

- Teaching the student to decode multisyllable words

- Providing strategies using mnemonics to remediate writing skills

- Instructing in appropriate use of a calculator for solving math problems

Considerations for Implementation

This intervention should be considered if data collected indicate that challenging behaviors occur because the child is lacking necessary academic skills to do instructional tasks (skill deficit). It may be useful to have an objective staff member other than the teacher conduct an informal evaluation of the student's skills to help determine whether the student knows how to do the task being presented.

Sample References

Sample references include Barton-Arwood, Wehby, and Falk (2005); Lane et al. (2008); and Strong, Wehby, Falk, and Lane (2004).

Problem-Solving Strategies

This intervention involves teaching specific strategies that allow a student to independently and successfully complete academic tasks or to succeed in various social interaction situations. The student may have basic academic and/or social skills but exhibits difficulty in more complex situations.

Uses

Consider using this intervention when the PTR assessment information indicates that challenging behavior occurs when

- The student is required to work independently or has difficulty staying engaged in the task.

- The student is attempting to complete a complex task.

- The student gets "stuck" while working on an academic task and does not know how to work through the difficulty alone.

- The student has a challenging interaction with a peer and does not know how to deal with it appropriately.

Examples

Examples include the following:

- Academic tasks (e.g., providing graphic organizers, using semantic maps, having a checklist to break complex tasks into small steps)

- Social interactions (e.g., dealing with teasing, ignoring, or walking away; reacting appropriately to peer pressure; identifying social and/or nonverbal cues)

Considerations for Implementation

Problem-solving strategies provide the student with a connection between knowledge they have already mastered and skills they need to acquire. Before implementation of this strategy, assess the student's current level of performance in the academic or social area targeted for instruction. To ensure successful performance, directly teach the problem-solving steps and provide immediate feedback to the student.

Sample References

Sample references include Erwin and Ruane (1993); Shure (1993); Webster-Stratton, Reid, and Hammond (2001).

General Coping Strategies

General coping strategies provide a student with self-control steps for dealing with conflicts.

Uses

Consider using this intervention when the PTR Assessment information indicates that

- The student has difficulty responding effectively to interpersonal or socially challenging situations.

- The student demonstrates an inability to control responses or reactions.

- The student becomes frustrated while engaged in academic tasks.

- The student is unable to communicate frustrations effectively or efficiently.

Examples

Examples include the following:

- Anger management

- Negotiation strategies

- Asking questions when frustrated

- Giving and accepting criticism

Considerations for Implementation

It is important to determine whether the student has a skill deficit (e.g., does not know how to cope with frustration) or a performance deficit (e.g., knows strategies for dealing with frustrating situations but does not use them). If it is a skill deficit, ensure that direct instruction of the behavior is provided with ample opportunities for guided and independent practice. If it is a performance deficit, providing an additional reinforcer that is powerful may be required to enhance the likelihood of the student using coping skills.

Sample References

Sample references include Kellner, Bry, and Colletti (2002); and Presley and Hughes (2000).

Specific Social Skills

This intervention involves teaching specific skills to enhance the social competence of students.

Uses

Consider using this intervention when the PTR assessment information indicates that

- Challenging behavior occurs because the student does not use appropriate social behaviors.

- The student knows appropriate behaviors, but does not always use them.

Examples

Examples include the following:

- Making conversation

- Accepting consequences

- Asking to join ongoing social activities

Considerations for Implementation

Skills targeted for instruction should be ones that can be learned quickly, used in multiple environments, and are powerful enough to get positive responses from others.

Sample References

Sample references include Gresham (2002); Gresham, Van, and Cook (2006); Jordan and Le Metais (1997); and Joseph and Strain (2003).

Teacher-Pleasing Behaviors

Teacher-pleasing behaviors are student behaviors that teachers perceive as important in the classroom.

Uses

Consider using this intervention when the PTR hypothesis indicates that

- The student demonstrates skill deficits for engaging in prosocial classroom or school behavior.
- The student possesses the skills to engage in socially appropriate behavior, but does not use the skills effectively.

Considerations for Implementation

This strategy should be considered if the intervention goals include

- Increasing rates of positive, prosocial behaviors within the classroom environment
- Increasing task productivity or engagement time
- Decreasing rates of inappropriate behavior

Examples

Examples include the following:

- Staying engaged in tasks
- Turning in high-quality work
- Being respectful of others' property
- Showing self-control

Considerations for Implementation

Determine whether the student has a skill-based or a performance deficit. If the student does not know how and when to perform the desired behaviors, use direct teaching methods for acquisition of new skills. If the student has the skills but does not perform them when necessary, determine appropriate reinforcement that will motivate the student to use teacher-pleasing behaviors.

Sample References

Sample references include Allday and Pakurar (2007) and Jenson et al. (1991).

Learning Strategies

Learning strategies are specific study skills and instructional strategies that help the student meet demands of multiple content area tasks. The major goals of learning strategies are to gain, respond to, and organize information.

Uses

Consider using this intervention when the PTR hypothesis indicates that

- The student has difficulty gathering relevant information from assigned materials.
- The student lacks learning strategies to meet the demands of content areas.
- The student is not generalizing learned skills to other classes or environments such as home or community.
- The student demonstrates difficulty with organizational skills and/or independent work.
- The student displays difficulty initiating effective study strategies.

Examples

Examples include the following:

- Skimming through reading material to find specific information
- Discriminating between important and unimportant information in texts
- Taking notes to study for a test

Considerations for Implementation

When developing learning strategies, determine the main content or main idea of the topic addressed, visual format, and process that will be taught to the student. Learning strategies are most effective when the content is organized and interpreted into forms that are learner friendly (i.e., easy to use and understand).

Sample References

Sample references include Falk and Wehby (2001); Fuchs et al. (2001, 2003); Hughes, Ruhl, Schumaker, and Deshler (2002); and Tralli, Colombo, Deshler, and Schumaker (1996).

Self-Management (Self-Monitoring)

This intervention provides a system in which the student monitors, evaluates, and reinforces his or her own performance or nonperformance of specified behaviors. Depending on the number of elements that are included, the intervention is referred to as *self-monitoring*, *self-reinforcement*, or *self-management*. All variations have been shown to be effective under certain circumstances.

Uses

Consider using this intervention when the PTR assessment information indicates that challenging behavior occurs when

- The student seeks to gain teacher or adult attention.
- The student seeks to escape an undesirable task or activity.
- The student attempts to delay a transition from a preferred to a nonpreferred activity.
- The student has academic demands placed on him or her.
- The student becomes frustrated during academic activities.

Example

Examples include the following:

- Providing the student a visual system to self-monitor target behaviors at prespecified time intervals

- Setting behavior performance goals to be achieved daily or weekly and having the student self-monitor progress toward reaching the goals

Considerations for Implementation

This strategy should be considered if intervention goal(s) include

- Increasing rates of positive behaviors such as attention to task or academic productivity

- Increasing task productivity

- Decreasing rates of inappropriate behavior

Appropriate recording and cuing systems should be selected that match the student's developmental level and preferences. The process of self-management should be clearly explained to the student. Before implementing the strategy, provide opportunities for the student to practice self-monitoring of behavior performance. The teacher may find role-modeling activities helpful to facilitate the student's understanding of when the target behavior is and is not performed and how to mark it on the self-management form. Feedback on the student's self-ratings as well as on behavior performance should be provided. If there is concern about the student's truthfulness in self-monitoring, the teacher should concurrently rate the behavior using a duplicate self-management form.

Sample References

Sample references include Carr and Punzo (1993); Dunlap, Dunlap, Koegel, and Koegel, 1991; Kern, Ringdahl, and Hilt (2001); Koegel, Koegel, Boettcher, Harrower, and Openden (2006); and Rock (2005).

Independent Responding

This intervention involves providing skills to the student, which allows him or her to answer questions without assistance from others.

Uses

Consider using this intervention when the hypothesis indicates challenging behavior occurs when

- The student wants to escape teacher or adult requests to respond independently or to complete a task.

- The student tries to gain assistance from staff or peers when required to respond independently or to complete a task without assistance.

- The student becomes frustrated during activities that require independent responses.

- The student is denied response assistance from an adult or peer.

Examples

Examples include the following:

- Teaching students to break assignments into parts and monitor their completion of the whole assignment
- Providing signals to assist the student in knowing when to provide responses
- Providing advanced preparation or scripts to give the student an increased chance of responding independently and correctly

Considerations for Implementation

When data indicate, this strategy should be considered for the student who is overly dependent on adults or peers to assist with tasks, or for the student who becomes frustrated when required to respond to academic questions.

Sample References

Sample references include Hughes, Ruhl, Schumaker, and Deshler (2002); and Tralli, Colombo, Deshler, and Schumaker (1996).

Increased Engagement Time

This intervention involves teaching the student strategies that will lengthen the amount of time that the student is attending to, and actively interacting in, the academic and social environments.

Uses

Consider using this intervention when the PTR assessment information indicates that

- The student exhibits low rates of engagement.
- The student has shown minimal academic growth.
- The student displays a need to learn self-management skills.
- The team sees the need for program change (e.g., presentation, materials, preferred topics) to motivate student to engage in academic tasks.

Examples

Examples include the following:

- Teaching and providing self-management systems
- Providing problem-solving or learning strategies that will motivate the student to remain engaged in an activity
- Using chaining and backward chaining to promote immediate success and as a tool to gradually increase engagement time

Considerations for Implementation

When data indicate, this strategy should be considered for the student who exhibits low rates of engagement and has shown minimal academic growth. When choosing this strategy, the team should consider appropriate prevention strategies (e.g., interspersing preferred topics or activities in materials, modifying curriculum content or presentations) that will motivate the student to be engaged in instructional tasks.

Sample References

Sample references include Lane, Weisenbach, Little, Phillips, and Wehby (2006); Liaupsin, Umbreit, Ferro, Urso, and Upreti (2006); Rock and Thead (2007).

Interventions for the Reinforce Component

This section describes interventions that should be considered for the Reinforce component of the behavior plan. The Reinforce replacement behaviors are marked with an asterisk (*) because the PTR Behavior Intervention Plan must include at least one Reinforce replacement behavior strategy to be a functionally derived intervention plan. For Reinforce strategies to be effective, they must do both of the following:

1. Occur following the appropriate replacement or desired behavior

2. No longer occur after the challenging behavior

The team should review the hypothesis of challenging behavior from Chapter 4 prior to selecting strategies from the following interventions. This will ensure that the strategies selected will reinforce the appropriate behavior and/or no longer reinforce the challenging behavior.

Reinforce Replacement Behavior (Functionally Equivalent)*

This intervention involves immediately providing the student's requested response when he or she engages in the functional replacement behavior selected from the Teach component.

Uses

This Reinforce strategy should be used whenever the student engages in the designated replacement behavior selected during the Teach component of the PTR intervention process. The replacement behavior serves the same function (obtain or escape) as the challenging behavior and is equally or more efficient and effective in obtaining the desired outcome (reinforcer) as the challenging behavior. It thus replaces the challenging behavior with a more appropriate and socially valid way of getting the original outcome.

Example

As soon as the student requests a break, a brief break from the activity should be given with minimal delay to the requested response. The student requests attention and the request is granted immediately by the teacher going to the student and saying, "Thank you for asking for attention appropriately. What do you need?"

Considerations for Implementation

Initially, the reinforcement (e.g., break, attention) should be given immediately after the student performs the replacement behavior. After the student is consistently engaging in the replacement behavior, a systematic plan for fading the immediacy and frequency of the reinforcement can be implemented. The Tolerance for Delay strategy is one way of doing this and is discussed later in this chapter. The Reinforcement of the Functionally Equivalent Replacement Behavior can be used simultaneously with Reinforcement of the Physically Incompatible Replacement Behavior that is described next.

Sample References

Sample references include Dufrene, Doggett, and Henington (2007); and Reichle and Johnston (1993).

Reinforce Replacement Behavior (Physically Incompatible)

This intervention involves providing the student with reinforcers contingent on the student performing the desired replacement behavior. A major criterion is that the power of the reinforcement for the desired behavior is of greater magnitude than the reinforcement for the challenging behavior. In some cases, it may be important to conduct a systematic assessment of potential reinforcers.

Uses

This Reinforce strategy should be used whenever the student exhibits the more appropriate, socially desirable replacement behavior, selected during the Teach component of the PTR intervention process. The reinforcer selected should be highly preferred (powerful) so that the student will be more likely to repeat the desired behavior.

Example

A student may get an extra 5 minutes at recess when he completes a math assignment, whereas asking for a break results in a brief 2-minute respite from the task.

Considerations for Implementation

When selecting effective reinforcers, it is helpful to review the student's current record of success of achieving a desired outcome after engaging in challenging behavior. In addition, the team should review whether the student has a history of being reinforced when a more appropriate behavior is performed. Often, students have learned that it is much more effective and efficient to avoid a task or to get a teacher's attention when they engage in challenging behavior than in appropriate behavior. For example, Emily has learned that when she calls out comments, the teacher responds to her much more quickly and consistently than when she raises her hand. Therefore, it is very important to guarantee that initially reinforcement is provided each time the student performs the desired behavior. If the team is concerned that this may not be possible due to time constraints or busy classroom schedules, the team should problem solve solutions. One option includes implementing the intervention in classroom routines in which the teacher has support and would have the time to provide immediate reinforcement to the student. Another option would be to modify the intervention to allow acknowledgment of the student's appropriate behavior with a signal or tally. For example, when Emily's teacher has a reading group and Emily is doing independent work at her desk, she often calls out for the purpose of getting the teacher's attention. The teacher wanted to replace Emily's call-outs with hand raising. However, the teacher knew that while she had a reading group, she would not be able to stop to acknowledge Emily's hand-raising behavior each time. Instead, she taught Emily to first get the teacher's attention by making eye contact prior to raising her hand. The teacher would acknowledge Emily's hand raise by showing her a "thumbs-up" and tallying the behavior's occurrence on a note card. After the reading group was completed, the teacher would go over to Emily and review her hand-raising behavior and deliver the agreed-on reinforcement for the behavior.

Sample References

Sample references include Halle, Bambara, and Reichle (2005) and Kern and Kokina (2008).

Discontinued Reinforcement of Challenging Behavior

This intervention involves no longer providing the response that followed and maintained the challenging behavior. The discontinued response should be the consequences identified during the reinforcement component of the assessment. For example, if the PTR Assessment information identified that challenging behavior typically resulted in teacher verbal reprimands and redirects, allowing the student to escape a task or to get attention, a different teacher-responding strategy will need to be implemented so that the student's challenging behavior will become ineffective in gaining the desired outcome. If the challenging behavior no longer "pays off" for the student, the occurrence of challenging behavior will lessen.

Uses

Consider using this intervention when the PTR assessment information indicates that the student's challenging behavior is maintained by

- The current adult response to the behavior (consequence)

- Adult attention, escape, delay or avoidance of a task or activity, or by gaining access to a desired item or activity

Example

When a student screamed, adults responded with emotion and escorted the student to time-out, thus delaying the start of the task. However, the assessment indicated that the student craves attention. Therefore, now when the student screams, the adults respond minimally (e.g., flat affect, minimal verbal responses, no eye contact).

Considerations for Implementation

No longer providing the desired outcome following a challenging behavior may not be feasible if the challenging behavior is dangerous to the student or others or if it is very disruptive to the classroom. Additionally, discontinuing reinforcement of challenging behavior may cause the challenging behavior to worsen. Many teachers find it difficult to stop responding to challenging behavior, thus making this Reinforce strategy difficult to implement. However, effectiveness is enhanced if the intervention plan includes strategies from the other core components (i.e., Prevent, Teach) and also includes a Teach Replacement Behavior strategy.

Sample References

Samples references include Braithwaite and Richdale (2000); Stahr, Cushing, Lane, and Fox (2006); and Sugai and Chanter (1989).

Group Contingencies

In the classical use of this intervention, a target behavior is required of a group of students and reinforcement is delivered contingent on the performance of the group. A modification of the group contingency by providing reinforcement to a group (e.g., the whole class) contingent on the individual student performing a required behavior can be very powerful in increasing the student's use of the new behavior.

Uses

Consider using this intervention when the PTR assessment information indicates that

- The student is reinforced by peer attention.

- Short-term goals include increasing peer interaction and friendship.

Examples

The teacher is concerned that the other students in the class may question the fairness of one student getting additional reinforcement that is not available to them.
Examples include the following:

- The class gets an ice cream party on Friday if Johnny reaches his goal of completing three out of five of his writing assignments for the week.

- The class gets bonus points toward a party each time Johnny reaches his self-management goal of staying engaged on a task.

Considerations for Implementation

Ideally, the reward should be based on the student engaging in a desired behavior rather than the absence of a challenging behavior. This encourages the student to demonstrate desired behaviors and provides a good link between engaging in those behaviors and the reward. It also is suggested that the class earn an extra reward rather than lose access to a reward. For example, the class should not lose minutes off recess if a student engages in a challenging behavior; rather, they should earn additional minutes if the student demonstrates the desired behavior. The contingency should focus on the positive completion of appropriate behavior. The team should decide how peers should respond when the student achieves the group reinforcement; likewise, the team should consider how to act when the student does not earn the reinforcement. Let's consider the case of Emily, from the previous Reinforcement strategy, who was being taught to raise her hand rather than call out. In Emily's intervention plan, the team decided that the class would earn an extra 10 minutes of recess outside once Emily had raised her hand 25 times. Twice per day, the teacher reviews Emily's progress toward the goal with the class. When she does achieve the goal, the teacher announces it and asks them to give Emily a round of applause. If she has not yet reached 25 hand raises, the teacher embeds a quick math activity by asking the class how many more times Emily needs to raise her hand prior to getting 25. She then asks the class to applaud Emily for getting closer to 25 hand raises. Designing the contingency in this way ensures that the student will get peer attention for appropriate behavior and not be ostracized or punished if the reinforcement is delayed. In Emily's case, the class will get the reinforcement. When Emily is having good days, the reinforcement will come more quickly than when she is having a less-than-good day.

Sample References

Sample references include Heering and Wilder (2006); Skinner, Skinner, and Sterling-Turner (2002); and Theodore, Bray, and Kehle (2004).

Increased Ratio of Positive to Negative Responses

This intervention involves responding positively to appropriate behavior exhibited by the student more often than responding negatively to inappropriate behavior.

Uses

Consider using this intervention when the PTR assessment information indicates that

- Adult's interactions with the student use a higher rate of negative statements (e.g., "no," "stop," "don't") for inappropriate behavior than positive statements in response to appropriate behavior (e.g., praise statements or comments about what the child is doing).

- The student engages in inappropriate behavior to get attention from adults.

- The student and the teacher have a negative or strained relationship.

Example

A teacher decides to provide a minimum of eight positive responses within a 20-minute period in which the student typically displays challenging behaviors. The teacher places eight poker chips in her left pocket and will be hypervigilant for display of appropriate behaviors from the student. Each time she makes a positive comment to the student (e.g., "you've been working hard"), one chip is moved to the right pocket. After 20 minutes, the teacher checks to ensure her goal has been met, moving all the chips from the left to the right pocket.

Considerations for Implementation

It is suggested that for every negative response to an inappropriate behavior, there should be four positive responses to appropriate behaviors. Reinforcing a desired response frequently increases the probability that response will be exhibited again. At first, this seems unnatural for many people, but with time it becomes routine. In addition, negative responses following inappropriate behavior have not been shown to be effective at reducing occurrences of inappropriate behavior, particularly if the behavior function is to obtain attention. This is an easy strategy that can be included with minimal effort in any behavior support plan.

Sample References

Sample references include Beaman and Wheldall (2000); Montague and Renaldi (2001); Shores, Jack, et al. (1993); and Stormont, Smith, and Lewis (2007).

Home–School Reinforcement System

In this intervention, a student earns reinforcement at home for behavior performed at school. This may be in addition to a school reinforcement system or as a stand-alone reinforcement system.

Uses

Consider using this intervention when the PTR assessment information indicates that

- The parent is actively involved with the process

- The child's highly preferred reinforcement is not available or usable at school

- Challenging behavior persists in the home setting and has an impact on behavior in the school setting

- Challenging behavior occurs specifically at transitions between home and school

Example

Joe's mother wanted to provide more powerful reinforcement to augment the PTR support plan. Because Joe loved to go to amusement parks, his mother agreed that Joe would earn a trip to the park every week he met his self-management goal. The teacher assisted Joe's mother in setting up a chart at home to show Joe how close he is in earning his trip to the park.

Considerations for Implementation

The student might earn points toward a powerful reinforcer provided at the end of the week, or small daily reinforcers might be used. Either plan should involve the student in the selection of the reinforcers. For some students this intervention may not be effective because the reward delay is too great. If used with a school reinforcement system, it is important that the parents and teacher communicate on a regular basis and the rules for the reinforcement system are consistent across home and school.

Sample References

Sample references include Galloway and Sheridan (1994) and Leach and Ralph (1986).

Delayed Gratification

This intervention involves teaching the student to wait a specified period of time before receiving a reinforcer. The strategy is used when the student is consistently using his or her new replacement behavior and rarely performing the challenging behavior.

Uses

Consider using this intervention when the PTR assessment information indicates that

- The student engages in specific, appropriate behavior, but at an unacceptable rate.

- The student is using the replacement or desired behavior with consistency and is no longer exhibiting the challenging behavior, but the teacher wants to initiate fading the reinforcement of the replacement behavior.

- The student appropriately seeks adult/peer attention, but at an excessive rate.

- The student engages in on-task behavior with reinforcement, but the intervention goal is to increase task-engagement time intervals and reduce extrinsic reinforcement.

Examples

Examples include the following:

- The student uses replacement behavior and is provided a delay signal (e.g., finger up indicating 1 second) or word (e.g., "wait") before being provided or released to the reinforcer.

- The student must earn a specified number of points, tokens, or checkmarks before receiving the reinforcer.

- The student is provided with a specified number of allowable behaviors each day with a gradual decrease over time (e.g., giving the student a certain number of "asking questions" passes).

Considerations for Implementation

This strategy should be considered if the student has been exhibiting the appropriate skills and receiving consistent reinforcement but now needs to have the reinforcement systematically and gradually faded. It also can be used when the student exhibits an appropriate behavior (e.g., raises hand), but does so at an unacceptable or unnecessary rate. When first implementing this strategy, the delay should be minimal (e.g., 1 second, one more problem) before being released to the reinforcer. After the brief delay is tolerated, gradually increase the delay (e.g., extend time to 2 seconds, then 3, and so forth; increase number of completed problems to 2, then 3, and so forth). By carefully planning the increases in the delay, the team should ensure that the student will continue to use the new replacement behavior. Do not sabotage the plan by trying to get the student to tolerate a longer delay than planned (e.g., after the student does one more problem, asking for completion of another problem). This may result in the student reverting back to using the challenging behavior to more effectively and efficiently achieve the desired outcome.

Sample References

Sample references include Hagopian, Contrucci Kuhn, Long, and Rush (2005); and Hagopian, Toole, Long, Bowman, and Lieving (2004).

Crisis Intervention Plan

This intervention is used for situations in which a student exhibits severe and/or intense behavior that puts themselves or others in danger. The intervention provides a temporary plan to calm the situation and keep all students and staff safe. A crisis plan is outside the scope of the PTR Behavior Intervention Plan in that it is to be used when immediate attention must be given to reestablishing stability to a situation rather than using it as a teachable moment. However, a crisis plan does fit the scope of the PTR behavior intervention plan in that it should be comprehensive, carefully developed and agreed on by the team, and ready to be used in the event that a crisis situation occurs. Doing so makes the crisis plan less of a reactive strategy (Bambara & Knoster, 2005). In addition, having a well-developed PTR Behavior Intervention Plan to address the student's challenging behaviors should ideally prevent situations in which a crisis plan will be needed. Before developing a crisis intervention plan, the team should obtain additional resources that describe specific crisis intervention approaches (e.g., deescalation procedures, Life Space Crisis Intervention, crisis prevention interventions) and seek the training essential to implement the interventions.

Uses

Consider using this intervention when the PTR assessment information indicates that

- The student's behavior has been dangerous or has a high probability of becoming dangerous

Example

The team develops a comprehensive crisis plan to respond to Joe when he begins to physically assault adults or peers in the classroom. The team determines the steps and responsibilities each person will have whenever the behavior occurs. The plan is written and placed in a spot that is easily accessed by all adults in the classroom.

Considerations for Implementation

Use of this plan simply reestablishes calm and stability in the environment. There has not been extensive research conducted on the effectiveness of crisis practices; therefore, the team should not rely on the plan to be the only intervention used to address challenging behavior. It should only be used during dangerous situations that are sudden and may have an impact on the entire classroom or school. Having a comprehensive PTR Behavior Intervention Plan will effectively address preventing challenging behaviors and increasing appropriate skills. Additional factors to consider include

- Proper training of staff to carry out the plan procedures effectively and efficiently

- Clear identification of team members and their roles

- Clear identification of challenging behavior situations that warrant initiation of the crisis plan

- Rehearsal of the plan during noncrisis times

- Response with minimal disruption to classroom activities

- Preparation to reinforce appropriate behaviors at a higher level and rate

- Verbal prompts and assurances to students to let them know they are safe

Sample References

Sample references include Brock, Lazarus, and Jimerson (2002); Brock, Sandoval, and Lewis (2001); Dawson (2003); DeMagistris and Imber (1980); Grskovic and Goetze (2005); and Pitcher and Poland (1992).

TIP

The interventions must match the hypothesis and be doable in the classroom. Ask the teacher, "Can you do this in the classroom with all your other responsibilities?"

PTR INTERVENTION CHECKLIST

Once team members have reviewed all of the interventions, they should use the PTR Intervention Checklist (see Appendix 5.1) to select possible strategies that will be considered. Team members should check the strategies they think fit best with the hypothesis *and* are feasible to be done by the teacher in the classroom. For an intervention to have the potential of being effective, it must be one that will actually be implemented. Thus, it is very important that the teacher and the team feel that the intervention can be done within the classroom. For example, if the team determines that based on the student's hypothesis, the Prevent Intervention of noncontingent reinforcement would be an effective strategy if attention is delivered every 2 minutes, but the teacher indicates that it would not be possible to deliver attention as often as designed, the team would need to discuss modifying the intervention or selecting an alternate strategy from the Prevent component that matches the hypothesis and can be done in the classroom context.

The PTR Intervention Checklist may be completed individually by each team member and discussed later as a team. Alternatively, the team may complete it together as a discussion guide for potential intervention strategies. When completing the checklist, the team should rank order between two and four strategies in each component (i.e., Prevent, Teach, and Reinforce) that they believe fit the hypothesis and are likely to be implemented in the classroom, for a total of 6–12 strategies. Remember, the team must teach the student a replacement behavior that will be performed in place of the challenging behavior, and they must reinforce the new behavior so that it will result in the same outcome as the challenging behavior. Therefore, the Replacement Behavior intervention under the Teach category and the Reinforce Replacement Behavior under the Reinforce category are mandated and must be included in the PTR Behavior Intervention Plan, even if the team gives these interventions a lower ranking order. Figure 5.1 shows a completed PTR Intervention Checklist for Rachel.

PTR INTERVENTION SCORING TABLE

If the team chooses to have each member complete the PTR Intervention Checklist independently, the PTR Intervention Scoring Table (see Appendix 5.2) should be used to rank all the interventions selected by the team. This can be done in several ways including computing a mean ranking score of each intervention selected, tallying the number of team members who gave a ranking to an intervention, or simply identifying which intervention

Hypothesis: *When* Rachel is given an independent writing assignment, she *will* get out of her seat, wander around the room, and talk to peers until the teacher sends her to the behavior specialist. ***As a result,*** she is able to **escape** her work and obtain **attention from the behavior specialist**.

Prevent	Rank	Teach	Rank	Reinforce	Rank
Providing choices (4: 1,1,1,2)	1	**Replacement behavior** Functionally equivalent (1:1) Physically incompatible (3: 1,1,1)	1*	**Reinforce replacement behavior** Functionally equivalent (1:1) Physically incompatible (3: 1,1,1)	1*
Curricular modifica-tions (4: 1,2,2,2)	2*	**Increased engagement time** (3: 2,2,3)	2	**Discontinue reinforcement of problem behavior** (3: 2,2,3)	2
Environmental supports (3: 3,3,4)	3	**Independent responding** (3: 2,3,3)	3	**Increase ratio + to –responses** (3: 2,3,3)	3

*Indicates teacher ranked intervention strategy as *1*.

Figure 5.2.   Rachel's PTR Intervention Scoring Table (see Appendix 5.2).

was ranked first most often, second most often, and third most often. Be sure to make note of which interventions the teacher selected because he or she will most likely be the person implementing the plan; thus, the teacher's ideas of what is feasible to be implemented in the classroom are very important. An example of Rachel's PTR Intervention Scoring Table is provided in Figure 5.2.

The example in Figure 5.2 uses the mean ranking score to prioritize the list of the interventions selected by Rachel's team members. The numbers within the parentheses following each intervention include the number of team members selecting the intervention and the rankings of each team member. For example, *Providing Choices* was selected by four team members. Three team members ranked the intervention as their first choice (i.e., 1), while one team member ranked it as their second choice (i.e., 2). The mean of the rank orders (i.e., sum of [1 + 1 + 1 + 2] / 4) is 1; thus, it is listed as the most preferred intervention of the team. However, note that no asterisk appears next to the rank order, indicating that the teacher did *not* rate this intervention as the top choice. In this example, the team should have facilitated discussion with the teacher to discuss whether he or she was willing and able to implement this intervention strategy in the classroom. If the teacher did not think the strategy was one that could be implemented, then the team should go to the top ranked intervention that was selected by the teacher, ensure that the strategy links to the hypothesis, and list it as the preferred intervention.

Once the team has come to consensus on the top-ranked intervention strategies in each component, they must agree on at least one Prevent, one Teach, and one Reinforce strategy that will be implemented and described in the PTR Behavior Intervention Plan. Again, it is very important that the team consider the intervention selections of the teacher (or whoever will be implementing the plan) in their final determination of the strategies selected. Once the team has identified at least three strategies, they should write a step-by-step behavior plan so that it is very clear how the behavior strategy will be implemented. It also is imperative that the team return to the PTR Behavior Rating Scale (BRS) developed in Chapter 3 to ensure that the replacement behavior identified by the team to be taught to the student is tracked on the BRS. If not, the teams should review the BRS procedure described in Chapter 3 to develop appropriate anchors for evaluating the student use of the replacement behavior once the intervention is implemented.

BEHAVIOR INTERVENTION PLAN

After reviewing the PTR Intervention Scoring Table and gaining consensus on the desired strategies to be used in the behavior plan, the team should task analyze each intervention to develop a step-by-step plan of implementation. A more specific plan will be easier for the teacher to implement.

The reinforcement strategy selected for Rachel (Reinforce Functional Replacement Behavior) allowed her to earn a brief break. To facilitate implementation of the intervention strategy, the specific steps of what Rachel's teacher should do were written out in detail. Table 5.1 contrasts a generic description of the intervention strategy with the specific, task-analyzed description. Although it does take more time up front to write the intervention with detailed specificity, it increases the likelihood that the teacher will understand how to implement the intervention and feel competent in performing the steps as written. It also ensures that the plan is written specifically for the target student in his or her environment rather than being a generic plan that could be implemented for any student. Finally, by thinking through each intervention strategy, the team will be able to identify any needed materials, resources, or potential limitations to be resolved before implementation.

The following questions may assist the team in developing a specific, step-by-step behavior intervention plan.

Prevent Questions

- Are additional materials or resources needed to implement the intervention (e.g., schedules, visual aids, charts, checklists, timers, books)?
- If so, who is going to develop those materials or obtain those resources?
- When will the intervention be implemented (e.g., the antecedent events identified in the PTR Assessment—transitions, arrival, math class, nonpreferred activities)?
- Are environmental or curricular modifications required?
- If so, who will make the modifications and how will they be presented to the student?
- Are specific peers needed to implement the intervention?
- If so, who will select, train, and reinforce the peers?

Table 5.1. Generic and specific behavior plans

Reinforce strategy	Generic behavior plan	Specific behavior plan
Reinforcing functional replacement behavior: asking for a break	When Rachel asks for a break, she will be allowed to take a 1-minute break.	When Rachel gives her break card to staff, she will be allowed to stop working on the activity for 1 minute.
		Staff will praise Rachel for using her break card and immediately release her to the break.
		Staff will remind Rachel that she may sit in her seat or walk around the perimeter of the room without talking to anyone.
		Staff will set the timer for 1 minute and remind Rachel that she may take a break until the timer goes off.

Teach Questions

- Has the replacement behavior been operationally defined?

- What specific skill(s) are needed to perform the replacement behavior? Does the student already have the skills? (Remember, the replacement behavior must be as easy for the student to perform as was the challenging behavior. If the replacement behavior requires the student to acquire new skills, the team should use shaping techniques, or reinforcing successive approximations to the desired new behavior.)

- Who is going to teach the replacement behavior?

- How and when will the replacement behavior be taught (e.g., modeling, role play, guided practice)?

- What specifically will the implementer say and/or do to carry out the intervention effectively (e.g., cues, prompts)?

- At what point in time does the teacher prompt the student to use the replacement behavior? (Remember, since the replacement behavior is performed rather than the challenging behavior, the team should review the PTR Assessment information to determine at what point in a problematic context the student displays the challenging behavior. The student should be prompted to use the replacement behavior immediately prior to the triggering event. For example, if the PTR Assessment determined that Joe starts screaming after the teacher gives him a demand to take out his math book, Joe should be prompted to use his replacement behavior of asking for a break immediately after the teacher gives the academic demand.)

Reinforce Questions

- What was the outcome of the challenging behavior? How will that same outcome be delivered to the student contingent on performance of the new replacement behavior? Will the new behavior get reinforced as quickly as did the challenging behavior? (Remember, the new skill must be more effective at getting the desired outcome [e.g., escape, obtain] than the challenging behavior.)

- What else is reinforcing to the student? What specific people, items, or activities are rewarding to the student?

- Are the reinforcers readily available?

- If not, what needs to happen so the reinforcers are available when needed?

- If the reinforcer is a person, will that individual always be available when needed (e.g., time with the physical education coach)?

- Who will provide the reinforcer?

- When will the reinforcer be delivered?

- How will delivery be tracked to ensure the reinforcer is provided?

> **TIP** *The behavior intervention plan should be a step-by-step description of how to implement the intervention strategies.*

It is essential that the team come to a consensus on at least one Prevent, one Teach, and one Reinforce strategy that are doable in the classroom and match the hypothesis developed in Chapter 4. Once the strategies are identified, the team should write the behavior intervention plan describing the specific steps that the implementer should follow. By

PREVENT Behavior Interventions

Intervention type	Specific steps
Curricular modification	To assist Rachel with correctly identifying letters to be capitalized, red ink will be used to identify letters to be capitalized and to identify the lines on the writing paper that the capital letters should touch. 1. Change top lines on the paper that capital letters should touch to red. 2. Change letters to be capitalized to red. 3. Provide Rachel with the modified paper and assignment. 4. Review with Rachel that the letters in red should touch with red lines of the paper.

TEACH Behavior Interventions

Intervention type	Specific steps
Functional replacement behavior—Ask for a break	To assist Rachel in obtaining a break from activities when needed, she will be taught to sign break. 1. Prior to writing, remind Rachel that she may take a break if she needs it. 2. Remind Rachel that she is to walk to the teacher quietly. 3. Have Rachel demonstrate the break sign quietly. 4. Remind Rachel that she may walk around the room quietly until the timer goes off. Have her practice if needed. 5. Remind Rachel that she may take a break at the onset of problem behavior.

REINFORCE Behavior Interventions

Intervention type	Specific steps
Reinforce functional replacement behavior—Ask for a break	To increase the likelihood that Rachel will ask for a break from activities when needed, she will be allowed to take a 2-minute break when she asks. 1. Immediately provide praise for asking for the break (e.g., "Thank you for asking for a break"). 2. Remind Rachel that she may walk around the room quietly for 2 minutes and that once the timer goes off she is to return to her seat. 3. Set the timer for 2 minutes. 4. Immediately release Rachel to her break. 5. Prompt Rachel to return to her seat once the timer goes off (if needed).

Figure 5.3. Rachel's PTR Behavior Intervention Plan (see Appendix 5.3).

using such specificity, the team increases the likelihood the plan will be successful. A highly specified plan for Rachel is shown in Figure 5.3. Appendix 5.4 is an alternate version of the PTR Behavior Intervention Plan.

IMPLEMENTING THE BEHAVIOR INTERVENTION PLAN: TRAINING AND TECHNICAL ASSISTANCE

Once the team has selected the PTR interventions and developed the student's individualized behavior intervention plan, training and technical assistance on how to implement the interventions should be provided to the teacher and all other team members who will be responsible for the plan. The team should decide who will receive the training (e.g., teacher, teaching assistant) and who will provide the training (e.g., the individual on the team with the most experience in behavioral principles and positive behavior support). At minimum, the team should select for training the person who will work with the student the most.

Before implementing the behavior intervention plan in the classroom, the teacher or the primary intervention agent needs to be trained in how to implement the plan. This often is done best without the student present or with the student but not when the other students are present. Training the teacher to do the plan before implementing it, with the student in the classroom, allows the teacher to feel comfortable with the steps of each strategy and will assist the teacher in executing the plan accurately within the context of the daily classroom events. Training on the plan should include direct instruction methods such as modeling, role playing, or practice sessions with the student. Feedback should be provided to the teacher on his or her performance as well as getting input from the teacher on his or her comfort level to perform the intervention with accuracy.

To assist the team with training, the team should develop a PTR Training Checklist (see Appendix 5.5) to measure the intervention agent's fidelity in implementing the plan. To develop the training checklist, the team should first review the step-by-step implementation plan for each intervention strategy. Then, the team should record it on the training checklist. During the training, the person providing the training should review the step-by-step plan with the intervention agent using the direct instruction methods listed in the checklist, and indicate the accuracy of the performance by circling *yes* or *no* in the appropriate column after each step.

Rachel's PTR Training Checklist is shown in Figure 5.4. Each step necessary for implementation is listed for each intervention. First, the team discussed how to implement the plan. That is, they discussed what the teacher will say and do when implementing the plan in the classroom. Next, they role played. The trainer took on the role of Rachel while the teacher walked through what she would say and do during typical classroom events. (This may need to occur several times before the teacher will score *yes* on each step.) Finally, the

Task Analysis of Intervention	Did the implementer complete the step?	
PREVENT Component: Curricular Modification		
1. Top writing paper lines printed in red	(Yes)	No
2. Letters to be capitalized printed in red	(Yes)	No
3. Reviewed modification strategy with Rachel	(Yes)	No
TEACH Component: Functional Replacement Behavior (ask for break)		
1. Reminded Rachel that she may ask for a break prior to giving writing assignment	(Yes)	No
2. Reviewed with Rachel how she is supposed to ask for a break	(Yes)	No
3. Reviewed with Rachel what she may do during a break	Yes	(No)
4. Reminded Rachel that she may ask for a break at first onset of problem behavior	(Yes)	No
REINFORCE Component: Functional Replacement Behavior (ask for break)		
1. Praise given when asked for break	Yes	(No)
2. Reminded of rules of break	(Yes)	No
3. Set timer	(Yes)	No
4. Break given immediately	(Yes)	No
TOTAL (# Yes / # Total)	9/11	
Percent Score	82%	

Figure 5.4.   Rachel's PTR Training Checklist (see Appendix 5.5).

team debriefed on any foreseen events that might challenge or be an obstacle to the implementation of the plan. At the end of the training session, the trainer should circle *yes* or *no* on the checklist to indicate whether the teacher was able to accurately implement the step.

If the teacher does not score 100% during training, the training should continue until the teacher is able to accurately implement each step. However, there may be times in which some steps may not be implemented with 100% accuracy. In these cases, the trainer and teacher have some options. They can decide to go ahead and implement the intervention with the student, and hopefully, with repeated practice and support, the teacher will perform the strategy competently. A second option is to determine the features of the strategy that may be difficult for the teacher to perform and decide if it can be modified to be more easily implemented. If the teacher cannot do the step with accuracy and it is an essential step, or if there are several steps of the specific strategy that are difficult to perform, the third option is to go back to the PTR Intervention Checklist and replace the strategy with a lower-ranked intervention that might be easier for the teacher to implement. In the case of Rachel's team, the teacher consistently forgot to review the rules of Rachel's break before giving her the writing assignment and to provide praise when a break was requested. In this case, the team decided that the steps were not critical to the success of the plan and might be strengthened with repeated practice and support while implementing the strategy with the student in the classroom context. The final training score obtained by Rachel's team was 82%.

TIP *First provide training to the teacher outside the normal classroom environment, then provide technical assistance and support in the classroom until the teacher is implementing the plan successfully.*

Once the teacher demonstrates fluent implementation of the interventions, technical assistance should be given to the teacher when the plan is implemented with the student in the classroom. Although the exact amount of technical assistance required cannot be predetermined, it is suggested that assistance be provided frequently at first and then faded as the teacher demonstrates accurate implementation of the plan (i.e., at least 80% accuracy). A schedule for providing the teacher technical assistance should be developed before implementation begins in the classroom to increase the likelihood that the support will be delivered. The first day that the teacher will be implementing the plan should be determined, and the team should make sure that the teacher is provided with support at that time. Being present on the first day of intervention is vital for several reasons. First, having someone else present when the teacher is attempting a new intervention can help the teacher feel more confident and comfortable because there is back-up support. Second, if the teacher has difficulty performing the intervention steps with fidelity, the person providing support can immediately assist or debrief with the teacher so that it is more likely the intervention will be implemented with fidelity. Third, if the intervention needs some modification to work in the classroom context, the person providing support and the teacher can problem solve and refine the strategy immediately.

When providing technical assistance, it is important to ask the teacher how he or she prefers to receive the assistance. Some teachers prefer to have the plan modeled for them. Others want to implement the plan first and then receive feedback on their implementation. However technical assistance is provided, it is important that the teacher receives feedback and changes are made to the plan as needed. The goal of technical assistance is to ensure that the teacher implements the plan with accuracy. Once this occurs, technical assistance can become less frequent and include more distal assistance via e-mail or telephone calls, until the student is meeting the goal(s) as identified by the team.

IMPLEMENTATION FIDELITY

After the team has developed a schedule for training and implementation, it is important to determine whether or not the interventions are being implemented consistently and correctly. Measuring the fidelity of how the intervention plan is being implemented is an extremely important part of the PTR process. The fidelity data will help the team make decisions on the effectiveness of the interventions. If the interventions are being implemented with high fidelity and data indicate a desired change in student behavior, the team can be more confident about the effectiveness of the intervention plan. However, if the data indicate little or no change in student behavior, the team will need to examine the fidelity data to determine the next step.

If there is little or no change in the student's behavior and the interventions are being implemented with low fidelity (i.e., inconsistently, inaccurately), the team must discuss whether and/or how the interventions need to be modified to ensure that the teacher implements them as designed. If, however, there is little or no change in the student's behavior and the interventions are being implemented with high fidelity (i.e., consistently and accurately), the team must determine how to modify the strategies to better match the hypothesis of challenging behavior. The team also may need to consider collecting additional data to more accurately identify the environmental events related to the challenging behavior.

TIP   *It is not uncommon for intervention agents to "drift away" from fidelity over time. Therefore, continuing to assess fidelity is essential.*

When developing a measure of fidelity, it is important to examine the intervention plan and identify the most critical steps of each intervention. Identifying the steps of each strategy makes it easier to recognize the components that must be evaluated on the fidelity measure. Most fidelity measures focus on two areas: adherence and quality. Adherence refers to the basic steps that must be implemented for the intervention plan to be effective. Quality focuses on how completely and correctly the steps are implemented; that is, are all the essential steps of the intervention being implemented with accuracy?

For example, in Rachel's plan, the strategy to *reinforce the replacement behavior: take a break* required the teacher to implement the following steps:

1. Provide praise when Rachel asks for a break.

2. Allow Rachel to take a break immediately on handing in her break card.

3. Remind Rachel of the rules of the break.

4. Set the timer for the break.

When measuring adherence of implementation for this strategy, the team would need to decide on the minimum step(s) required to ensure intervention implementation (i.e., is the teacher doing the strategy?). In this example, the team initially determined that the teacher should allow Rachel to take a break immediately when she asked. This would be the minimum step needed to ensure the strategy is being implemented; without this step, no intervention is occurring. However, after continued discussion, the teacher expressed concern that Rachel may refuse to return to her work after the break was over. The team then decided it was imperative that the timer be set to help prevent Rachel from refusing to return to work, or to cue her back to the assignment when the break ended. Both steps—allowing the break and setting the timer—were then needed to ensure adherence of implementation.

When measuring the quality of implementation for this strategy, Rachel's team determined that the teacher must implement all four of the intervention steps. That is, the teacher should not only give Rachel a break immediately on request, but the teacher must also provide praise for asking for a break, remind Rachel of the break rules, and set the timer. Only by completing all four of the steps would the teacher be rated as implementing the strategy with quality.

Measuring the adherence (i.e., are the minimum components of the intervention strategy being implemented?) versus the quality (i.e., how well is the plan being implemented?) should be a team decision that is based on the data and the needs of the student. Data might tell the team that even though the teacher is implementing only the minimum steps of the plan, the student is making progress; thus, it might not be necessary to implement each step. Additionally, as the student becomes fluent in the new skills, it may no longer be necessary to implement every step of the plan. For example, once Rachel has learned the break procedure (i.e., asking for a break always results in a break, she must return to her seat at the end of the break, and she may ask for a break whenever she needs it), it may no longer be necessary to review the rules of the break or set the timer every time Rachel takes a break. Thus, it is important for the team to use the data, as well as their judgments, to determine if and when changes to the behavior intervention plan and fidelity measures should be made.

TIP *In coaching staff on fidelity, it is critical to let them know from the outset that improvement is not the goal. Precise implementation is the goal.*

Regardless of what the team decides in terms of how well the plan is being implemented, it is imperative that the team at least measure the specific step(s) needed to have an intervention strategy in place. The team will then be able to make data-based decisions regarding the effectiveness of the behavior plan. If the teacher is implementing the plan with high fidelity but the student's behavior is not changing, the team can use the data to decide if the plan needs to be implemented more accurately (i.e., quality, measuring how well the plan is being implemented) or if new interventions are needed.

It is suggested that fidelity of implementation be measured each time technical assistance is provided in the classroom, especially during the first few weeks of implementation. Doing so provides the team with the data needed to make decisions regarding the effectiveness of the plan. Furthermore, some teachers find it helpful to use a checklist to monitor their own fidelity of implementation on a daily basis. The Fidelity of Implementation form (see Appendix 5.6) should be used to measure the fidelity of implementation. It will allow the team to identify the adherence and the quality of implementation. Again, the team should define adherence and quality based on the particular intervention strategy selected, the needs of the student, and the data.

Figure 5.5 provides a sample fidelity measure for Rachel's behavior intervention plan. Rachel's team used the form each time technical assistance was provided in the classroom. The team member who was skilled in implementing and providing training on behavior intervention plans conducted an observation during times when challenging behavior was most likely to occur and the behavior intervention plan was being implemented (e.g., during writing assignments). The observer tracked whether or not the teacher implemented the steps listed on the form. While observing writing on Monday, the teacher gave the modified writing paper to Rachel but did not review it with her, so the observer circled *Y* for adherence and *N* for quality. During the observation, Rachel stayed engaged and did not exhibit challenging behavior. Thus, there was no opportunity for either the replacement behavior or the reinforce strategy to occur. *NA* therefore was circled for the respective adherence and quality measures. The final step was to tally the number of *Y*s and *N*s to gain percentage scores for adherence, quality, and an overall fidelity implementation score.

Intervention strategy	Adherence— At a minimum, is it being implemented?	Quality— How well is it being implemented?	Intervention strategy score (add Ys then divide by Ys + Ns)
Curricular modification	Lines of writing paper and letters to be capitalized changed to red	Reviewed purpose of colored lines and letters with student	1/2 = .50
	(Y) N NA	Y (N) NA	
Replacement behavior—Ask for a break	Prompted student to ask for a break at first sign of problem behavior	Prompted student to ask for a break prior to writing activity	NA
	Y N (NA)	Y N (NA)	
Reinforce replacement behavior—Ask for a break	Allowed to take a break immediately and set timer	Allowed to take a break immediately, reminded of rules, timer set, and provided praise	NA
	Y N (NA)	Y N (NA)	
	Total adherence score (add Ys then divide by Ys + Ns)	**Total quality score** (add Ys then divide by Ys + Ns)	**Total fidelity score** (add total scores)
	1/1 = 1.0	**0/1 = 0.0**	**1/2 = 0.50**

Figure 5.5. Rachel's PTR Fidelity of Implementation (see Appendix 5.6).

SUMMARY

An effective PTR plan is one that includes input from all team members. However, the teacher's input should carry the greatest importance in determining which interventions will be implemented and how those strategies will look in the teacher's classroom. Ensuring contextual fit heightens the likelihood that the teacher will be vested in implementing the interventions. In addition, task analyzing the steps of each intervention in the behavior support plan will facilitate the teacher's implementation and provide consistency if multiple school personnel are implementing the PTR interventions. Finally, providing training, support, and technical assistance to the teacher and evaluating fidelity of implementation will enhance the likelihood of the teacher carrying out the interventions as intended and will allow the team to determine the effectiveness of the PTR Behavior Intervention Plan.

Appendix

5

PTR Intervention Checklist

Directions:

1. After reading the summaries of the interventions in Chapter 5, review your hypothesis statement on the PTR Functional Behavior Assessment Summary Table from Chapter 4.

2. Select the interventions that match the information in your hypothesis. Please select *at least two interventions* but *no more than four* in each category (Prevent, Teach, Reinforce). The interventions marked with asterisks are required and must be selected.

3. Rank order the selected interventions by placing a *1* in the box next to the most highly preferred, a *2* next to the second most preferred, and a *3* next to the third most preferred.

Student _____   **School** _____

Date _____   **Completed by** _____

Hypothesis _____

_____

_____

PREVENT Interventions	**TEACH Interventions**	**REINFORCE Interventions**
__ Providing choices	****Replacement Behavior**	****Reinforce Replacement Behavior**
__ Transition supports	__ Functionally equivalent	
__ Environmental supports	__ Physically incompatible	__ Functionally equivalent
		__ Physically incompatible
__ Curricular modification (eliminating triggers)	__ Specific academic skills	
__ Adult verbal behavior (just be nice)	__ Problem-solving strategies	__ Discontinue reinforcement of problem behavior
__ Classroom management		__ Group contingencies (peer, teacher)
	__ General coping strategies	__ Increase ratio of + to − responses
__ Increase noncontingent reinforcement	__ Specific social skills	__ Home-to-school reinforcement system
__ Setting event modification	__ Teacher-pleasing behaviors	__ Delayed gratification
__ Opportunity for prosocial behavior (peer support)	__ Learning skills strategies	
__ Peer modeling or peer reinforcement	__ Self-management (self-monitoring)	
	__ Independent responding	
	__ Increased engaged time	

Does the severity or intensity of the student's problem behavior pose a threat to self or others?   ❏ Yes ❏ No

If yes, is a crisis intervention plan needed?   ❏ Yes   ❏ No

**All interventions marked with asterisks need to be selected and included in the student's PTR intervention plan.

Appendix 5.2.

PTR Intervention Scoring Table

Directions:

1. Gather all completed PTR Intervention Checklists (see Appendix 5.1).

2. List the interventions ranked first, second, and third by each team member until all interventions are listed.

3. Determine the mean rank of all interventions selected.

4. List the interventions in order of rank.

5. Place an asterisk next to the interventions selected as *1* (one) by the teacher.

6. As a team, discuss the ranked interventions and come to a consensus on at least one Prevent, one Teach, and one Reinforce strategy.

Student _____ **School** _____

Date _____ **Completed by** _____

Hypothesis _____

_____

_____

_____

Prevent	Rank	Teach	Rank	Reinforce	Rank
1.		1. **Replacement behavior** ❏ Functionally equivalent ❏ Physically incompatible		1. **Reinforce replacement behavior** ❏ Functionally equivalent ❏ Physically incompatible	
2.		2.		2.	
3.		3.		3.	
4.		4.		4.	
5.		5.		5.	
6.		6.		6.	
7.		7.		7.	

A replacement behavior must be included in the student's PTR Behavior Intervention Plan.

PTR Behavior Intervention Plan

Directions:

1. Write the hypothesis developed in Chapter 4 on the top of the Behavior Intervention Plan.

2. List the Prevent intervention strategy in the appropriate *Intervention type* box.

3. Write a step-by-step plan for implementation of the Prevent intervention.

   a. When writing the step-by-step plan, think about each step the intervention agent should perform while implementing the plan. Be as specific as possible.

   b. It also might be helpful to write exactly what the teacher is to say (or provide examples).

   c. List where materials should be kept, when materials should be given to the student, and the number of materials to be given, for example.

   d. List each step the student is to perform.

4. Repeat steps 2 and 3 for all remaining intervention strategies.

Student _____ **School** _____

Hypothesis _____

_____

_____

PREVENT Behavior Interventions

Intervention type	Specific steps

TEACH Behavior Interventions

Intervention type	Specific steps

REINFORCE Behavior Interventions

Intervention type	Specific steps

PTR Behavior Intervention Plan (alternate version)

Directions:

1. Write the hypothesis developed in Chapter 4 on the top of the Behavioral Intervention Plan.

2. List the Prevent intervention strategy in the *Prevent interventions* column.

3. Write a step-by-step plan for implementation of the Prevent intervention.

   a. When writing the step-by-step plan, think about each step the intervention agent should perform while implementing the plan. Be as specific as possible.

   b. It also might be helpful to write exactly what the teacher is to say (or provide examples).

   c. List where materials should be kept, when materials should be given to the student, and the number of materials to be given, for example.

   d. List each step the student is to perform.

4. Indicate any comments that might be helpful in implementation or resources needed in the Comments box.

5. Repeat steps 2–4 for all remaining intervention strategies.

Student _____   **School** _____

Hypothesis_____

_____

_____

PREVENT interventions	TEACH interventions	REINFORCE interventions	Comments

Appendix 5.5. PTR Training Checklist

Directions for developing the form:

1. Select an intervention and write it next to the appropriate component.
2. As a team, use the specific, step-by-step Behavior Intervention Plan to identify the steps to be performed. Write one step in each box.
3. Repeat steps 1 and 2 for the remaining interventions.

Directions for completing the form:

1. Conduct training during a time when students are not present.
2. As a team, discuss the steps of implementation.
3. Next, use direct instruction methods to practice each step (i.e., role play, modeling, feedback).
4. Circle *Yes* if the intervention agent (i.e., person implementing the plan) correctly implements step(s).
5. Circle *No* if the intervention agent does not correctly implement step(s).
6. Calculate the percent score.
7. If the percent score is less than 100%, the team should discuss if further training is needed or develop a plan to ensure the weak steps are addressed during technical assistance.

Student _____

Intervention agent _____

Date of training _____

Task Analysis of Intervention	Did the implementer complete the step?	
PREVENT Component		
1.	Yes	No
2.	Yes	No
3.	Yes	No
4.	Yes	No
5.	Yes	No
6.	Yes	No
TEACH Component		
1.	Yes	No
2.	Yes	No
3.	Yes	No
4.	Yes	No
5.	Yes	No
6.	Yes	No
REINFORCE Component		
1.	Yes	No
2.	Yes	No
3.	Yes	No
4.	Yes	No
5.	Yes	No
6.	Yes	No
TOTAL (# Yes / # Total of Y and N)		
Percent Score		

Appendix 5.6.

PTR Fidelity of Implementation

Directions for developing the form:

1. Select an intervention and write it in the *Intervention strategy* box.
2. As a team, use the specific, step-by-step Behavior Intervention Plan to identify the minimal steps needing to be performed for the intervention to exist. Write the step(s) in the *Adherence* box.
3. As a team, use the specific, step-by-step Behavior Intervention Plan to identify the additional steps needing to be performed for the intervention to have the greatest effect. Write the step(s) in the *Quality* box.
4. Repeat steps 1–3 for the remaining interventions.

Directions for completing the form:

1. Observe during a time when the Behavior Intervention Plan is being implemented *and* problem behavior is likely to occur.
2. Select Yes if the intervention agent (i.e., person implementing the plan) correctly implements step(s).
3. Select No if the intervention agent does not correctly implement step(s).
4. Select NA if, at the end of the observation, the intervention agent did not have the opportunity to implement step(s) because the event did not occur (e.g., student did not use replacement behavior, choice strategy applies to reading and observation occurred during math).
5. Calculate intervention strategy, total adherence, total quality, and total fidelity scores by adding up the respective Yes scores and dividing by the respective Yes plus No scores.

Student _____   **Intervention agent** _____

Recorder _____   **Date** _____

Intervention strategy	Adherence—At a minimum, is it being implemented?	Quality—How well is it being implemented?	Intervention strategy score Y / Y = 2 Y / N = 1 N / N = 0 NA / NA = NA
	Y N NA	Y N NA	
	Y N NA	Y N NA	
	Y N NA	Y N NA	
	Y N NA	Y N NA	
	Y N NA	Y N NA	
	Total adherence score (add Ys then divide by Ys + Ns)	**Total quality score** (add Ys then divide by Ys + Ns)	**Total fidelity score** (Total Ys / Total Ys + Ns across adherence and quality)

Evaluation

OVERVIEW AND OBJECTIVES

The evaluation process is the final essential step of the Prevent-Teach-Reinforce (PTR) model. In this step, the team will establish a system to monitor the implementation of the intervention plan and identify a method for evaluating the student's progress. Once the intervention plan has been developed and is implemented within the classroom, it is important to continue collecting outcome data to determine whether the interventions are effective. The information obtained through the evaluation process allows the team to make data-based decisions regarding changes or additions that may need to occur to the intervention plan, as well as effectively address additional concerns or situations that may arise for the student.

Chapter 6 focuses on the following objectives:

- Determining a method for monitoring intervention implementation

- Identifying a system to evaluate the student's behavior changes

- Establishing a process to make data-based decisions

TIP

Team members are often overwhelmed by evaluation and data requirements; however, the behavior rating scale (BRS) system has been found to be easy to use and quite valuable. It is important to point out that BRS data can be used for purposes beyond the PTR process. The data can be used to supplement individualized education program teaching, home–school communication, and teachers' efficacy.

MONITORING AND EVALUATING BEHAVIOR RATING SCALE DATA

It is extremely important to collect data to know whether or not the intervention plan is successful in creating effective and appropriate behavior changes for the student. Within the PTR model, the Behavior Rating Scale (BRS), developed and implemented in Chapter 3, is initially used to collect baseline data. However, this tool also is used to obtain postintervention (outcome) data during the evaluation process. Outcome data are assessed by the team to determine if the targeted behaviors are improving, remaining the same, or getting worse. The team should use the BRS outcome data to determine the effectiveness of the intervention plan, but they also can combine this information with the PTR Fidelity of Implementation scores (see Appendix 5.6) to assist them in making the most accurate and appropriate decisions regarding the entire intervention process. To aid the team in understanding how to measure, review, and evaluate outcome data, a case example and BRS samples are provided to illustrate several outcomes that might be obtained for a student.

Consider a student, Tyrone, who exhibited screeching behavior, which was extremely disruptive to the learning environment. After discussion and brainstorming, the team determined that Tyrone's screeching was his most significant behavior problem. However, they also expressed concern about his lack of academic progress due to excessive off-task behavior. Following the steps in the PTR model, the team developed goals for Tyrone and discussed how best to use the BRS to collect data on the screeching and academic engagement. They established anchor points for each of the behaviors and began collecting baseline data. Next, they completed a functional assessment, determined a data-based function for the screeching behavior, and developed a hypothesis regarding Tyrone's challenging behavior. With the hypothesis in mind, appropriate interventions were selected by the team to target the screeching and off-task behaviors, and an intervention plan detailing the strategies chosen was developed. The teacher and other key team members were trained on how to implement the intervention strategies effectively. With the implementation of the intervention plan, the team continued to collect BRS data to determine the effectiveness of the strategies and make ongoing data-based decisions regarding next steps. The BRS in Figure 6.1 represents positive postintervention data for Tyrone's screeching and on-task behavior.

When assessing the BRS, the team first reviewed the baseline data—i.e., those scores obtained prior to the implementation of the intervention plan. The team did this for two important reasons. First, the team needed to ensure they had selected behaviors that were truly significant and problematic for the student. Second, they needed to make sure the anchor points accurately reflected the severity of the chosen behaviors. Tyrone's BRS baseline data indicated that he was engaging in approximately 16–20 screeching incidents per day with a mean score of 4.2, which the team agreed was significant and extremely disruptive to the learning environment. The baseline data for academic engagement illustrated that Tyrone remained on task between 20% and 29% (BRS mean = 1.8) of the day with 1 day being estimated at less than 20%, which the team determined was extremely low and, therefore, in need of intervention.

TIP   *When the data indicate that the plan is effective, all staff involved should be reinforced for their efforts. Celebrate!*

Next, the team evaluated the student's postintervention data—that is, the information obtained after the intervention strategies were implemented. Tyrone's postintervention data on the BRS showed a consistent decrease in his screeching behavior and a consistent increase in his academic engagement. By the end of the 2 weeks of intervention implementation, Tyrone was engaging in screeching 5 times or less per day (BRS mean = 2.6) compared with the 16–20 times per day during baseline. His on-task behavior improved from 20% to 29% during baseline to 40% or more by the end of the second week (BRS mean = 3.4)

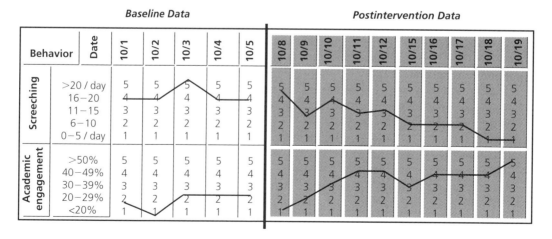

Figure 6.1. Tyrone's Behavior Rating Scale: Positive change data.

		Baseline Data					Postintervention Data									
Behavior	Date	10/1	10/2	10/3	10/4	10/5	10/8	10/9	10/10	10/11	10/12	10/15	10/16	10/17	10/18	10/19
Screeching	>20 / day	5	5	5	5	5	5	5	5	5	5	5	5	5	5	5
	16–20	4	4	4	4	4	4	4	4	4	4	4	4	4	4	4
	11–15	3	3	3	3	3	3	3	3	3	3	3	3	3	3	3
	6–10	2	2	2	2	2	2	2	2	2	2	2	2	2	2	2
	0–5 / day	1	1	1	1	1	1	1	1	1	1	1	1	1	1	1
Academic engagement	>50%	5	5	5	5	5	5	5	5	5	5	5	5	5	5	5
	40–49%	4	4	4	4	4	4	4	4	4	4	4	4	4	4	4
	30–39%	3	3	3	3	3	3	3	3	3	3	3	3	3	3	3
	20–29%	2	2	2	2	2	2	2	2	2	2	2	2	2	2	2
	<20%	1	1	1	1	1	1	1	1	1	1	1	1	1	1	1

Figure 6.2. Tyrone's Behavior Rating Scale: Stable data pattern.

By comparing the BRS baseline data points to postintervention data points, this example clearly demonstrates that the intervention being implemented resulted in a change in Tyrone's behaviors, and his performance was poised to reach the team's desired goals. The data collected on Tyrone's screeching behavior indicates a decrease in the number of screeching incidents per day and the academic engagement data demonstrates that Tyrone was increasing his academic engaged time throughout the day. In addition, the mean scores obtained in baseline and postintervention can be compared to determine the plan's impact on behavior change. In Tyrone's case, his screeching behavior decreased from a baseline mean rating of 4.2 to a postintervention mean rating of 2.6. Academic engaged time showed a post-test intervention mean rating of 3.4, an improvement over the baseline mean rating of 1.8. These data verified to the team that the targeted behaviors were improving and the intervention strategies were effective in addressing the behaviors of concern.

However, BRS outcome data may not always demonstrate positive behavior changes. In some cases, the data may indicate a lack of improvement toward the team's desired goals for the student. Figure 6.2 shows an example of a stable pattern with minimal movement of data points from baseline to postintervention. In this scenario, Tyrone engaged in screeching behavior during baseline between 16 and 20 times per day for an average BRS score of 4.2. However, after implementing the intervention strategies, the postintervention data show that Tyrone continued to engage in the screeching behavior at about the same frequency as baseline, with an average BRS score of 4.3. The same was true for Tyrone's on-task behavior. During baseline, Tyrone engaged in on-task behavior approximately between 20% and 29% of the time (BRS mean = 1.8). Once the intervention plan was put in place, Tyrone's academic engagement scores remained fairly stable, with his time on task averaging about the same as it did in baseline (BRS mean = 1.9).

Finally, BRS data may indicate that the behaviors of concern are deteriorating. If the targeted behaviors are not improving, the data will show a trend in the opposite direction of the desired goals. The BRS in Figure 6.3 is an example of a data pattern showing behavior worsening after intervention. The baseline data for Tyrone's screeching indicated that the behaviors were typically occurring between 16 and 20 times each day. However, the postintervention data indicate that the screeching incidents increased slightly to more than 20 times per day. In addition, Tyrone engaged in on-task behavior between 20% and 25% of the day during baseline. Once the intervention plan implemented, Tyrone's on-task behavior showed a noticeable decline to less than 20% of the day. A comparison of the mean rating scores from baseline to postintervention confirm that the behavior is not showing the

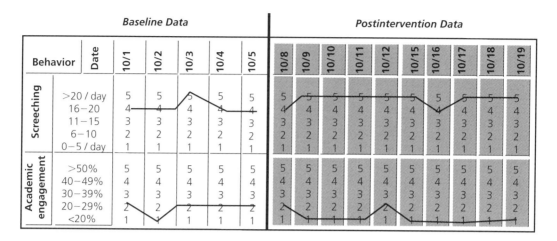

Figure 6.3. Tyrone's Behavior Rating Scale: Declining data pattern.

desired improvement. Screeching behavior had a mean postintervention BRS rating of 4.8 compared to 4.2 at baseline while academic engagement mean rating decreased from a baseline score of 1.8 to a postintervention mean of 1.2. These data clearly illustrate that the intervention plan was not moving Tyrone's behaviors in the desired direction.

TIP   *At a minimum, the team should review the postintervention data every 2 weeks.*

MAKING DATA-BASED DECISIONS: BEHAVIORS ARE IMPROVING

TIP   *Behavior improvement does not signal the termination of the plan, only a change in focus from skill acquisition to mastery and maintenance.*

Improvements in a student's targeted behaviors, such that challenging behaviors are decreasing and replacement and/or desired behaviors are increasing (as illustrated in Figure 6.1 for Tyrone), are good reasons for a team to celebrate. However, behavior improvements should not cause the team to stop implementing the intervention plan. Even if the BRS data indicate the student's behaviors are improving and he or she is moving toward the desired goals, the team's next step is to brainstorm strategies to ensure that the student moves from acquisition level to mastery and finally to maintenance—just as they would if academic skills were being addressed. Depending upon the breadth and depth of the interventions, the team may consider several avenues for reaching goal mastery and maintenance.

Extension

One way to move the student from acquisition to mastery to skill maintenance is to extend the scope of the intervention plan. If the plan is being implemented in only one routine or setting, the team may want to expand the plan so that generalization, and eventually mastery, of the desired new skills is fostered. Extending the plan may involve implementing the intervention in a second routine or another environmental setting. Plan extension also may include teaching a new interventionist to implement the strategies (e.g., another teacher, paraprofessional, parent). To extend the scope of the intervention plan, the team should use the same processes described in Chapters 2–5 to determine the expanded goals, develop appropriate BRS anchor points, modify the intervention plan if necessary, and train individuals to implement the refined strategies. Finally, the team should develop a technical assistance and monitoring plan to support implementation and review data to determine whether the intervention retains effectiveness.

Shaping

If the intervention plan is already being implemented throughout the day or in multiple settings, the team may choose to change the BRS anchor points in an attempt to shape the student's target behavior. This modification is warranted for situations in which the team's desired goal includes behaviors that the student did not have in his or her current repertoires. For example, Johnny's tantrum behaviors before intervention typically lasted between 4 and 5 minutes. Although the team wanted Johnny to have no tantrums or tantrums of very short duration (e.g., 10 seconds or less), the team knew that initially it would be difficult for Johnny to achieve this goal. They decided that a reasonable goal would be to initially decrease the tantrums to 1–2 minutes in duration. After implementing the intervention for 3 weeks, postintervention data suggested that Johnny's tantrums, on average, had decreased to a duration of 2–3 minutes, with the trend being relatively stable. The team then decided to change the reasonable goal to zero duration (i.e., absence of tantrums) and make the respective changes to the other anchors. The behavior intervention plan would be changed to deliver reinforcement contingent on the lower duration of tantrum behavior. When using the shaping strategy, it is important for the team to clearly define the ultimate behavioral goal (the behavior NOT currently in the student's repertoire) and the initial behavioral goal. In addition, they may need to operationalize the intermediate steps between the initial behavioral goal and the final desired behavioral goal. For example, in Johnny's case the final desired goal was the absence of tantrums (0 seconds duration). The initial behavioral goal was 1–3 minutes duration. Intermediate steps could include 1–2 minutes; 1 minute; less than 1 minute; and, finally, 0 seconds duration. Each time the team changes the anchor points and behavioral targets, a vertical line should be drawn on the BRS immediately prior to the first date of establishment of the new anchor points to allow for accurate comparison and evaluation of the changes in the student's behaviors using the new criteria.

Fading Reinforcement

A third strategy for moving the student from acquisition to mastery to skill maintenance is to fade reinforcers. However, before fading reinforcement, the team should review the data to confirm that the student is using the new behavior or skill (teaching intervention) consistently and that the challenging behavior has been extinguished or reduced to an acceptable level. If the data establish that both of these factors are occurring, a plan for fading reinforcement can be developed. The team may choose to fade reinforcers by decreasing the frequency of delivery. For example, the teacher can provide the reinforcer every other time the student exhibits the desired behavior rather than every time or every third time it is displayed (e.g., using an intermittent fixed ratio reinforcement schedule rather than a continuous reinforcement schedule). Another method for fading reinforcers is to use delayed gratification (see Chapter 5). Delayed gratification entails teaching the student to wait a specified period of time, complete a certain amount of work, and/or exhibit a specific number of desired behaviors before receiving the reinforcer.

Self-Management

Finally, the team may develop a self-management system when the BRS data show steady behavioral progress toward the desired goals. A self-management or self-monitoring strat-

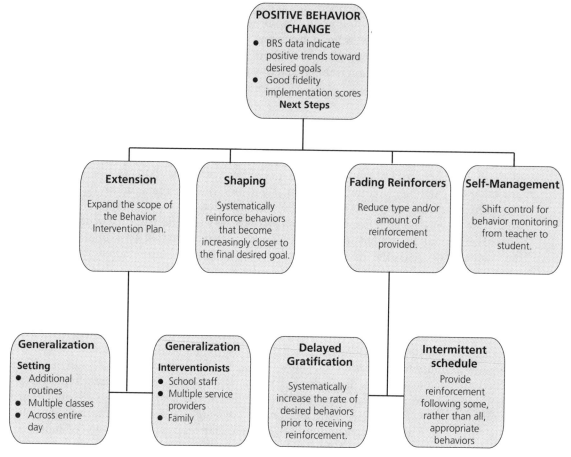

Figure 6.4. Skill mastery to maintenance: Decision-making tree. BRS, Behavior Rating Scale.

egy provides the student with a system to monitor, evaluate, and reinforce his or her own performance of specific behaviors. Such a system allows the student more ownership of the intervention strategies and fosters greater independence. Figure 6.4 may assist the team in determining the next steps when moving a student from skill acquisition to mastery, and ultimately to maintenance, based on the data.

Case Example

Johnny is a first-grade student in a general education classroom. His teacher is concerned about his tantrums and minimal academic progress. She and the behavior specialist meet and decide to address Johnny's behavior using PTR. A team is created and together they complete the next three steps in the PTR process, which include goal setting and data collection, functional assessment, and the development and implementation of a behavior intervention plan. During the goal-setting and data collection step, the team determines that Johnny's most significant behaviors of concern are his tantrums, which also affect his academics. They develop operational definitions and anchor points for the behaviors. The teacher begins collecting baseline data using the BRS on the frequency of tantrums and amount of time Johnny remains on task during academic activities.

Next, the team completes a functional assessment. Based on the functional behavior assessment data, the team decides the teacher will implement the plan only during reading because that activity was identified as the most problematic routine. The assessment data also indicate that when Johnny is required to complete nonpreferred academic tasks, the occurrence of challenging behaviors increases. The team hypothesizes that the function of Johnny's tantrums is to escape/avoid nonpreferred tasks. They develop an intervention plan based on the hypothesis, which includes choice making for the Prevent component, a request for a break for the Teach component, and the release to a short 1-minute break as the Reinforce component. In addition, when Johnny engages in the desired behavior, he can spend the last 10 minutes of the reading period in a preferred activity such as computer or a board game. The teacher is trained on how to accurately implement each of the strategies and begins implementing the intervention plan with Johnny.

During the first week of implementation, BRS data indicate that Johnny is making consistent improvement toward his desired goals of decreasing tantrums and increasing time on task. The teacher likes the interventions, gives high ratings to their social validity, and indicates the interventions are easy to implement in the classroom. Data obtained from the fidelity implementation checklist observations reveal that the teacher is implementing the interventions accurately and completely and needs minimal coaching support. Because Johnny is responding well to the interventions during reading, the teacher and team decide to extend the scope of the intervention plan by implementing the strategies during math class, a time in which Johnny continues to engage in tantrums. The hypothesis previously developed for the tantrum behavior matches the events in math; therefore, the team determines that the current interventions can be used with only slight modifications.

One week after implementing the interventions during math, the team meets to review the evaluation data. Johnny's behavior shows consistent improvements during math, and the gains made during reading have been maintained. The team decides to start fading the break by using the delayed gratification strategy. Now, when Johnny requests a break, the teacher will ask him to work for 30 more seconds (delay signal), after which time she will then release him to his break. After 5 days of Johnny successfully working for 30 more seconds, the teacher will increase the delay to 60 seconds, and thus continually and gradually increase the delay until Johnny is able to stay engaged for the majority of the academic work time. Each week, the team will meet to review the BRS data to ensure that behavior improvements continue to be maintained.

It is important to note that some strategies may always need to be in place for certain students. For example, a team may determine that a student's independent work activities are too difficult and trigger challenging behavior anytime they are presented to the student. Thus, the independent activities serve as a trigger that inevitably results in the occurrence of challenging behavior. An appropriate prevention intervention might include a curricular modification to address the difficulty level of the tasks. Unless the student is able to acquire the necessary skills so that the content is no longer perceived as difficult, the curricular modification may always need to be in place to prevent challenging behavior from occurring. This is particularly relevant for students with learning difficulties who need remedial supports or individualized education program services.

MAKING DATA-BASED DECISIONS: NO BEHAVIOR IMPROVEMENT

In situations in which there is no change in behavior, the team should first review the Fidelity of Implementation checklist to ensure that the interventions were implemented in the manner intended. If the fidelity scores are low, the team should discuss what intervention features make it difficult for the teacher or others to implement the strategies. Some features contributing to low fidelity scores might include

- Interventions that are more difficult to implement than originally thought

- Insufficient time for the teacher to plan and prepare the intervention strategies

- Unrealistic time requirements for the teacher to implement the plan

- The need for additional supports and/or resources

If the team determines the intervention plan is being implemented with low fidelity because the strategies are too difficult or the teacher has insufficient time to plan, prepare, and/or implement the interventions, the team may want to consider redesigning or modifying the strategies to make them more feasible for classroom use. The team should use the fidelity data and any additional data collected to determine which features of the interventions appear to be the primary obstacles hindering successful implementation.

TIP   *Any additional interventions selected must match the hypothesized function of the behavior determined during the functional behavior assessment process.*

If the team decides to select different interventions, the PTR Intervention Checklist summary (see Chapter 5), completed earlier in the process, should be reviewed. The team can consider implementing one or more of the other interventions selected by the teacher (e.g., the #2 or #3 ranked interventions under each category) by determining their match with the hypothesis and the likelihood of the teacher accepting and using the strategy. If the other strategies ranked do not match the hypothesis or are not interventions that the teacher will be willing to implement, the team can have each member rank-order new interventions under each category, keeping in mind that at least one type of Teach Replacement Behavior and Reinforce Replacement Behavior must be included in any PTR intervention plan. Any new interventions selected and agreed on by the team will need to be task analyzed, and the teacher must be trained to implement the strategies as described previously with follow-up support provided to the teacher. Fidelity measures should be conducted on implementation of the new strategies, and BRS data must be collected. Remember, when the plan is changed in any way, a new vertical line should be drawn on the BRS immediately before the date the revised plan was implemented. This line allows the team to evaluate the impact the changes have on student behavior.

If fidelity scores are acceptable, the team should evaluate the intervention plan to determine if there is a need for any modifications or changes. For example, if the timing of prompting for the replacement behavior appears to occur too late (e.g., challenging behavior occurs before the student is prompted to use the new skill), a minor adjustment in the delivery of the instructional prompt may enhance the effectiveness of the strategy. Finally, the PTR Assessment information and hypothesis should be revisited to make sure that the function suggested by the team is indeed the primary purpose of the challenging behavior or that the contextual events under which behavior occurs are accurate. For example, the team may have hypothesized that Cindy's cussing behavior was for attention. They implemented a Teach (Functionally Equivalent) Replacement Behavior strategy that prompted Cindy to request attention rather than cursing. After implementing the strategy for 5 days, the BRS data indicated that Cindy's cussing behavior was getting worse. The team reviewed the PTR Assessment data and hypotheses and decided that Cindy's behavior was primarily to avoid or escape nonpreferred tasks, with attention being a secondary outcome. They modified the behavior plan by teaching an escape replacement behavior (e.g., asking for a 1-minute "chill" time) and added a Reinforce strategy that provided enriched attention when Cindy chose to engage in her nonpreferred task without cursing. After implementing the modified strategy, Cindy's cursing behavior decreased and her engagement in nonpreferred tasks began to increase.

It is extremely important for the team to continuously review the BRS data and the fidelity scores from the implementation checklist throughout the PTR process. This information allows the team to make data-based decisions for continuing, discontinuing, or changing interventions. Using this data, the team will be able to document areas of weakness within the plan, evaluate student progress toward the desired goals, identify interventions that may require supplemental training and/or technical assistance to help the teacher achieve greater accuracy of implementation, and determine next steps toward skill mastery and maintenance.

Figure 6.5 can assist the team in determining next steps if the BRS data indicate the student's behavior problems are not improving,

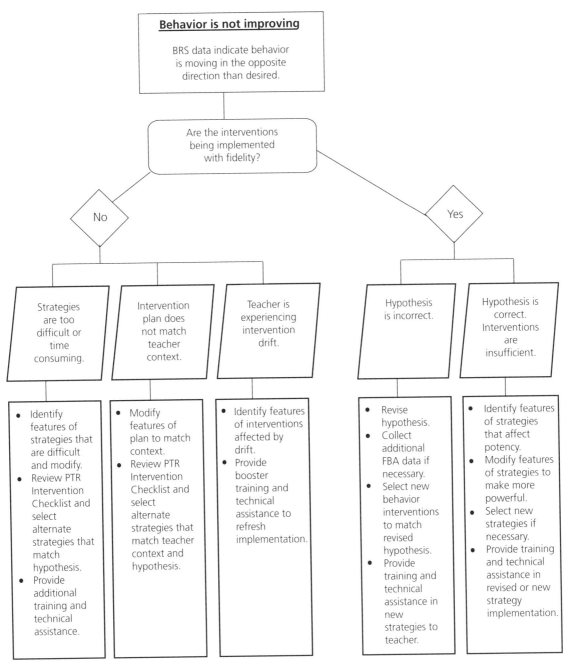

Figure 6.5. Determining the next steps. BRS, behavior rating scale; FBA, functional behavior assessment.

SOCIAL VALIDITY

While it is vital to monitor the impact of the intervention on the student, it is equally important to determine whether the teacher found the intervention plan acceptable and effective. Interventions with high social validity have a greater likelihood of being adopted by teachers for continued use. An example of a teacher Social Validity Scale, adapted from Reimers and Wacker (1988), is available in Appendix 6.1 and the accompanying CD. The team may choose to use this form to gain information from the teacher and/or other intervention agents regarding the effectiveness and acceptability of the intervention plan developed by the team. The social validity measure should not be used until the teacher has been implementing the strategies for at least 2 weeks.

SUMMARY

It is extremely important to continually monitor the implementation of the intervention plan and evaluate all available data. This allows the team to determine the effectiveness of the intervention plan, evaluate the student's responses to the strategies, document the teacher's fidelity of implementation, and verify areas for change. The PTR Behavior Intervention Plan and Fidelity of Implementation checklist are good tools for ongoing data monitoring and evaluation. The data obtained using these measures will guide the team in asking pertinent questions and making sound data-based decisions.

Appendix

6

Appendix 6.1 PTR Self-Evaluation: Social Validity

PTR Self-Evaluation: Social Validity

Directions: Please score each item by circling the number that best indicates how you feel about the PTR intervention(s).

1. Given this student's behavior problems, how acceptable do you find the PTR behavior plan?

1	2	3	4	5
Not at all acceptable		Neutral		Very acceptable

2. How willing are you to carry out this behavior plan?

1	2	3	4	5
Not at all willing		Neutral		Very willing

3. To what extent do you think there might be disadvantages in following this behavior plan?

1	2	3	4	5
None likely		Neutral		Many likely

4. How much time will be needed each day for you to carry out this behavior plan?

1	2	3	4	5
Little time will be needed		Neutral		Much time will be needed

5. How confident are you that the behavior plan will be effective for this student?

1	2	3	4	5
Not at all confident		Neutral		Very confident

6. How likely is this behavior plan to make permanent improvements in this student's behavior?

1	2	3	4	5
Unlikely		Neutral		Very likely

7. How disruptive will it be to carry out this behavior plan?

1	2	3	4	5
Not at all disruptive		Neutral		Very disruptive

8. How much do you like the procedures used in the proposed behavior plan?

1	2	3	4	5
Do not like them at all		Neutral		Like them very much

(Page 1 of 2)

From the *Treatment Acceptability Rating Form–Revised (TARF-R)*, © 1988 by T. Reimers & D. Wacker; adapted by permission.

In *Prevent-Teach-Reinforce: The School-Based Model of Individualized Positive Behavior Support* by G. Dunlap, R. Iovannone, D. Kincaid, K. Wilson, K. Christiansen, P. Strain, & C. English. (2010, Paul H. Brookes Publishing Co., Inc.)

9. How willing will other staff members be to help carry out this behavior plan?

1	2	3	4	5
Not at all willing		Neutral		Very willing

10. To what extent are undesirable side effects likely to result from this behavior plan?

1	2	3	4	5
No side effects likely		Neutral		Many side effects likely

11. How much discomfort is this student likely to experience during this behavior plan?

1	2	3	4	5
No discomfort at all		Neutral		Very much discomfort

12. How willing would you be to change your routines to carry out this behavior plan?

1	2	3	4	5
Not at all willing		Neutral		Very willing

13. How well will carrying out this behavior plan fit into the existing routine?

1	2	3	4	5
Not at all well		Neutral		Very well

14. How effective will the intervention be in teaching your student appropriate behavior?

1	2	3	4	5
Not at all effective		Neutral		Very effective

15. How well does the goal of the intervention fit with the team's goals to improve the student's behavior?

1	2	3	4	5
Not at all		Neutral		Very much

Addendum to Social Validity: Do you have any additional comments to make about the intervention and its effect on the student and/or the class? For example, are other students now making additional social invites to the student, or does the student seem to do better in other routines not targeted for the intervention?

(Page 2 of 2)

In *Prevent-Teach-Reinforce: The School-Based Model of Individualized Positive Behavior Support* by G. Dunlap, R. Iovannone, D. Kincaid, K. Wilson, K. Christiansen, P. Strain, & C. English. (2010, Paul H. Brookes Publishing Co., Inc.)

References

Allday, R.A., & Pakurar, K. (2007). Effects of teacher greetings on student on-task behavior. *Journal of Applied Behavior Analysis, 40,* 317–320.

Appley, D.G., & Winder, A.E. (1977). An evolving definition of collaboration and some implications for the world of work. *Journal of Applied Behavioral Science, 13,* 279–291.

Armendariz, F., & Umbreit, J. (1999). Using active responding to reduce disruptive behavior in a general education classroom. *Journal of Positive Behavior Interventions, 7,* 152–158.

Bambara, L., & Kern, L. (Eds.). (2005). *Individualized supports for students with problem behaviors: Designing positive behavior plans.* New York: Guilford Press.

Bambara, L.M., & Knoster, T. (2005). Designing positive behavior support plans. In M. Wehmeyer, L. Michael, & M. Agran (Eds.), *Mental retardation and intellectual disabilities: Teaching students using innovative and research-based strategies* (pp. 149–174). Auckland, New Zealand: Pearson Education New Zealand.

Barton-Arwood, S.M., Wehby, J.H., & Falk, K.B. (2005). Reading instruction for elementary-age students with emotional and behavioral disorders: Academic and behavioral outcomes. *Exceptional Children, 72,* 7–27.

Beaman, R., & Wheldall, K. (2000). Teachers' use of approval and disapproval in the classroom. *Educational Psychology, 20,* 431–446.

Braithwaite, K.L., & Richdale, A.L. (2000). Functional communication training to replace challenging behaviors across two behavioral outcomes. *Behavioral Interventions, 15,* 21–36.

Brock, S.E., Lazarus, P.J., & Jimerson, S.R. (Eds.). (2002). *Best practices in school crisis prevention and intervention.* Bethesda: National Association of School Psychologists.

Brock, S.E., Sandoval, J., & Lewis, S. (2001). *Preparing for crises in the schools: A manual for building school crisis response teams* (2nd ed.). New York: Wiley.

Carr, E.G. (1988). Functional equivalence as a mechanism of response generalization. In R.H. Horner, G. Dunlap, & R.L. Koegel (Eds.), *Generalization and maintenance: Lifestyle changes in applied settings* (pp. 221–241). Baltimore: Paul H. Brookes Publishing Co.

Carr, E.G., Dunlap, G., Horner, R.H., Koegel, R.L., Turnbull, A.P., Sailor, W., et al. (2002). Positive behavior support. Evolution of an applied science. *Journal of Positive Behavior Interventions, 4,* 4–16.

Carr, E.G., Horner, R.H., Turnbull, A.P., Marquis, J., Magito-Mclaughlin, D., McAtee, M.L., et al. (1999). *Positive behavior support for people with developmental disabilities: A research synthesis.* Washington, DC: American Association on Mental Retardation.

Carr, J.E., Coreaty, S., Wilder, D.A., Gaunt, B.T., Dozier, C.L., Britton, L.N., et al. (2000). A review of noncontingent reinforcement as treatment for aberrant behavior of individuals with developmental disabilities. *Research in Developmental Disabilities, 21,* 377–391.

Carr, S.C., & Punzo, R.P. (1993). The effects of self-monitoring of academic accuracy and productivity on the performance of students with behavioral disorders. *Behavioral Disorders, 18,* 241–250.

Clarke, S., Dunlap, G., & Vaughn, B. (1999). Family-centered, assessment-based intervention to improve behavior during an early morning routine. *Journal of Positive Behavior Interventions, 1,* 235–241.

Cole, C.L., Davenport, T.A., Bambara, L.M., & Ager, C.L. (1997). Effects of choice and task preference on the work performance of students with behavior problems. *Behavioral Disorders, 22,* 65–74.

Colvin, G., Sugai, G., & Patching, W. (1993). Pre-correction: An instructional strategy for managing predictable behavior problems. *Intervention in School and Clinic*, *28*, 143–150.

Cooper, J.O., Heron, T.E., & Heward, W.L. (2007). *Applied behavior analysis.* Upper Saddle River, NJ: Pearson Merrill/Prentice Hall.

Cooper, L.J., Wacker, D.P., Thursby, D., Plagmann, L.A., Harding, J., Millard, T., et al. (1992). Analysis of the effects of task preferences, task demands, and adult attention on child behavior in outpatient and classroom settings. *Journal of Applied Behavior Analysis*, *25*, 823–840.

Cote, C.A., Thompson, R.H., & McKerchar, P.M. (2005). The effects of antecedent interventions and extinction on toddlers' compliance during transitions. *Journal of Applied Behavior Analysis*, *38*, 235–238.

Cushing, L.S., & Kennedy, C.H. (1997). Academic effects of providing peer support in general education classrooms on students without disabilities. *Journal of Applied Behavior Analysis*, *30*, 139–150.

Darch, C.B., & Kameenui, E.J. (2003). *Instructional classroom management: A proactive approach to behavior management* (2nd ed.). White Plains, NY: Longman.

Dawson, C.A. (2003). A study on the effectiveness of Life Space Crisis Intervention for students identified with emotional disturbances. *Reclaiming Children and Youth*, *11*, 223–230.

DeMagistris, R.J., & Imber, S.C. (1980). The effects of life space interviewing on academic and social performance of behaviorally disordered children. *Behavioral Disorders*, *6*, 12–25.

Doggett, A.R., Edwards, R.P., Moore, J.W., Tingstrom, D.H., & Wilczynski, S.M. (2001). An approach to functional assessment in general education classroom settings. *School Psychology Review*, *30*, 313–328.

Dooley, P., Wilczenski, F.L., & Torem, C. (2001). Using an activity schedule to smooth school transitions. *Journal of Positive Behavior Interventions*, *3*, 57–61.

Duchnowski, A.J., & Kutash, K. (2009). Integrating PBS, mental health services, and family-driven care. In W. Sailor, G. Dunlap, G. Sugai, & R. Horner (Eds.), *Handbook of positive behavior support* (pp. 203–231). New York: Springer.

Dufrene, B.A., Doggett, R.A., & Henington, C. (2007). Functional assessment and intervention for disruptive classroom behaviors in preschool and Head Start classrooms. *Journal of Behavioral Education*, *16*, 368–388.

Dunlap, G. (2006). The applied behavior analytic heritage of PBS: A dynamic model of action-oriented research. *Journal of Positive Behavior Interventions*, *8*, 58–60.

Dunlap, G., & Carr, E.G. (2007). Positive behavior support and developmental disabilities: A summary and analysis of research. In S.L. Odom, R.H. Horner, M. Snell, & J. Blacher (Eds.), *Handbook of developmental disabilities* (pp. 469–482). New York: Guilford Press.

Dunlap, G., Carr, E.G., Horner, R.H., Zarcone, J., & Schwartz, T.R. (2008). Positive behavior support and applied behavior analysis: A familial alliance. *Behavior Modification*, *32*, 682–698.

Dunlap, G., Iovannone, R., Wilson, K., Kincaid, D., & Strain, P. (in press). Prevent-Teach-Reinforce: A standardized model of school-based behavioral intervention. *Journal of Positive Behavior Interventions*.

Dunlap, L.K., Dunlap, G., Koegel, L.K., & Koegel, R.L. (1991). Using self-monitoring to increase students' success and independence. *TEACHING Exceptional Children*, *23*(3), 17–22.

Eber, L., Hyde, K., Rose, J., Breen, K., McDonald, D., & Lewandowski, H. (2009). Completing the continuum of schoolwide positive behavior support: Wraparound as a tertiary-level intervention. In W. Sailor, G. Dunlap, G. Sugai, & R. Horner (Eds.), *Handbook of positive behavior support* (pp. 671–703). New York: Springer.

Ervin, R., Radford, P., Bertsch, K., Piper, A., Ehrhardt, K., & Poling, A. (2001). A descriptive analysis and critique of the empirical literature on school-based functional assessment. *School Psychology*, *30*, 193–210.

Erwin, P.G., & Ruane, G.E. (1993). The effects of a short-term social problem solving program with children. *Counseling Psychology Quarterly*, *6*, 317–323.

Falk, K.B., & Wehby, J.H. (2001). The effects of peer-assisted learning strategies on the beginning reading skills of young children with emotional or behavioral disorders. *Behavioral Disorders*, *26*, 344–359.

French, N.K. (2002). *Managing paraeducators in your school: How to hire, train, and supervise non-certified staff.* Thousand Oaks, CA: Corwin Press.

Fuchs, D., Fuchs, L.S., Thompson, A., Svenson, E., Yen, L., Otaiba, S.A., et al. (2001). Peer-assisted learning strategies in reading: Extensions for kindergarten, first grade, and high school. *Remedial and Special Education, 22,* 15–21.

Fuchs, L.S., Fuchs, D., Prentice, K., Burch, M., Hamlett, C.L., Owen, R., et al. (2003). Enhancing third-grade student mathematical problem solving with self-regulated learning strategies. *Journal of Educational Psychology, 95,* 306–316.

Galloway, J., & Sheridan, S.M. (1994). Implementing scientific practices through case studies: Examples using home-school interventions and consultation. *Journal of School Psychology, 32,* 385–413.

Gillies, R.M., & Ashman, A.F. (1997). The effects of training in cooperative learning on differential student behavior and achievement. *Journal of Classroom Interaction, 32,* 1–10.

Gresham, F.M. (2002). Teaching social skills to high-risk children and youth: Preventive and remedial strategies. In M. Shinn, H. Walker, & G. Stoner (Eds.), *Interventions for academic and behavior problems II: Preventive and remedial strategies* (pp. 403–432). Bethesda, MD: National Association of School Psychologists.

Gresham, F.M., Van, M.B., & Cook, C.R. (2006). Social skills training for teaching replacement behavior: Remediating acquisition deficits in at-risk students. *Behavioral Disorders, 31,* 363–377.

Grskovic, J.A., & Goetze, H. (2005). Evaluation of the effects of Life-Space-Crisis Intervention on the challenging behavior of individual students. *Reclaiming Children and Youth, 13,* 231–235.

Hagopian, L.P., Contrucci Kuhn, S.A., Long, E.A., & Rush, K.S. (2005). Schedule thinning following communication training: Using competing stimuli to enhance tolerance to decrements in reinforcer density. *Journal of Applied Behavior Analysis, 38,* 177–193.

Hagopian, L.P., Toole, L.M., Long, E.S., Bowman, L.G., & Lieving, G.A. (2004). A comparison of dense-to-lean and fixed-lean schedules of alternative reinforcement and extinction. *Journal of Applied Behavior Analysis, 37,* 323–338.

Halle, J., Bambara, L.M., & Reichle, J. (2005). Teaching alternative skills. In L. Bambara & L. Kern (Eds.) *Individualized supports for students with problem behaviors: Designing positive behavior plans* (pp. 237–274). New York: Guilford Press.

Hanley, G.P., Iwata, B.A., & McCord, B. (2003). Functional analysis of problem behavior: A review. *Journal of Applied Behavior Analysis, 36,* 147–186.

Heering, P.W., & Wilder, D.A. (2006). The use of dependent group contingencies to increase on-task behavior in two general education classrooms. *Education & Treatment of Children, 29,* 459–468.

Hughes, C.A., Ruhl, K.L., Schumaker, J.B., & Deshler, D.D. (2002). Effects of instruction in an assignment completion strategy on the homework performance of students with learning disabilities in general education classes. *Learning Disabilities Research & Practice, 17,* 1–18.

Ingram, K., Lewis-Palmer, T., & Sugai, G. (2005). Function-based intervention planning: Comparing the effectiveness of FBA function-based and non-function-based intervention plans. *Journal of Positive Behavior Interventions, 7,* 224–236.

Iovannone, R., & Dunlap, G. (2001). Assessment-based curricular interventions for challenging behavior. *Autism-Asperger's Digest,* September–October, 14–16.

Iovannone, R., Greenbaum, P., Wei, W., Kincaid, D., Dunlap, G., & Strain, P. (in press). Randomized control trial of a tertiary behavior intervention for students with problem behaviors: Preliminary outcomes. *Journal of Emotional and Behavioral Disorders.*

Iwata, B.A., Dorsey, M., Slifer, K., Bauman, K., & Richman, G. (1982). Toward a functional analysis of self-injury. *Journal of Applied Behavior Analysis, 27,* 197–204.

Jenson, W.R., Christopulos, K., Zimmerman, M., Nicholas, P., Reavis, K., & Rhode, G. (1991). A much needed link with regular education: The generalization of behaviorally disordered students. *The Oregon Conference Monograph,* 115–121.

Jones, K.M., Drew, H.A., & Weber, N.L. (2000). Noncontingent peer attention as treatment for disruptive classroom behavior. *Journal of Applied Behavior Analysis, 33,* 343–346.

Jones, K.M., Young, M.M., & Friman, P.C. (2000). Increasing peer praise of socially rejected delinquent youth: Effects on cooperation and acceptance. *School Psychology Quarterly, 15,* 30–39.

Jones, V.F., & Jones, L.S. (2001). *Comprehensive classroom management: Creating communities of support and solving problems* (6th ed.). Boston: Allyn & Bacon.

Jordan, D.W., & Le Metais, J. (1997). Social skilling through cooperative learning. *Educational Research, 39,* 3–21.

Joseph, G.E., & Strain, P.S. (2003). Comprehensive evidence-based social emotional curricula for young children: An analysis of efficacious adoption potential. *Topics in Early Childhood Special Education, 23*(2), 65–76.

Kellner, M.H., Bry, B.H., & Colletti, L. (2002). Teaching anger management skills to students with severe emotional or behavioral disorders. *Behavioral Disorders, 27,* 400–407.

Kennedy, C.H., & Itkonen, T. (1993). Effects of setting events on the problem behavior of students with severe disabilities. *Journal of Applied Behavior Analysis, 26,* 321–327.

Kern, L., & Clemens, N.H. (2007). Antecedent strategies to promote appropriate classroom behavior. *Psychology in the Schools, 44,* 65–75.

Kern, L., Delaney, B., Clarke, S., Dunlap, G., & Childs, K. (2001). Improving the classroom behavior of students with emotional and behavioral disorders using individualized curricular modifications. *Journal of Emotional and Behavioral Disorders, 9,* 239–247.

Kern, L., & Kokina, A. (2008). Using positive reinforcement to decrease challenging behavior. In J. Luiselli, D.C. Russo, W.P. Christian, & S.M. Wilczynski (Eds.), *Effective practices for children with autism: Educational and behavior support interventions that work* (pp. 413–432). New York: Oxford University Press.

Kern, L., Ringdahl, J.E., & Hilt, A. (2001). Linking self-management procedures to functional analysis results. *Behavioral Disorders, 26,* 214–226.

Koegel, L.K., Koegel, R.L., Boettcher, M.A., Harrower, J., & Openden, D. (2006). Combining functional assessment and self-management procedures to rapidly reduce disruptive behavior. In R.L. Koegel & L.K. Koegel (Eds.), *Pivotal response treatments for autism: Communication, social, and academic development* (pp. 245–258). Baltimore: Paul H. Brookes Publishing Co.

Kohler, F.W., & Strain, P.S. (1992). Applied behavior analysis and the movement to restructure schools: Compatibilities and opportunities for collaboration. *Journal of Behavioral Education, 2,* 367–390.

Lambert, M.C., Cartledge, G., & Heward, W.L. (2006). Effects of response cards on disruptive behavior and academic responding during math lessons by fourth-grade urban students. *Journal of Positive Behavior Interventions, 8,* 88–99.

Lane, K.L., Harris, K.R., Graham, S., Weisenbach, J.L., Brindle, M., & Morphy, P. (2008). The effects of self-regulated strategy development on the writing performance of second-grade students with behavioral and writing difficulties. *The Journal of Special Education, 41,* 234–253.

Lane, K.L., Rogers, L.A., Parks, R.J., Weisenbach, J.L., Mau, A.C., Merwin, M.T., et al. (2007). Function-based interventions for students who are nonresponsive to primary and secondary prevention efforts: Illustrations at the elementary and middle school levels. *Journal of Emotional and Behavioral Disorders, 15,* 169–183.

Lane, K.L., Weisenbach, J.L., Little, M.A., Phillips, A., & Wehby, J. (2006). Illustrations of function-based interventions implemented by general education teachers: Building capacity at the school site. *Education and Treatment of Children, 29,* 549–571.

Larson, C.E., & LaFasto, F. (1989). *Teamwork: What must go right/what can go wrong.* Newbury Park, CA: Sage Publications.

Leach, D.J., & Ralph, A. (1986). Home-school reinforcement: A case study. *Behaviour Change, 3,* 58–62.

Liaupsin, C.J., Umbreit, J., Ferro, J.B., Urso, A., & Upreti, G. (2006). Improving academic engagement through systematic, function-based intervention. *Education and Treatment of Children, 29,* 573–591.

Lohrmann, S., & Talerico, J. (2004). Anchor the boat: A class-wide intervention to reduce problem behavior. *Journal of Positive Behavior Interventions, 6,* 113–120.

Luiselli, J.K. (Ed.). (2006). *Antecedent assessment and intervention: Supporting children and adults with developmental disabilities in community settings.* Baltimore: Paul H. Brookes Publishing Co.

Matheson, A.S., & Shriver, M.D. (2005). Training teachers to give effective commands: Effects on student compliance and academic behaviors. *School Psychology Review, 34,* 202–219.

McLaughlin, D.M., & Carr, E.G. (2005). Quality of rapport as a setting event for problem behavior: Assessment and intervention. *Journal of Positive Behavior Interventions, 7,* 68–91.

Mesibov, G.B., Browder, D.M., & Kirkland, C. (2002). Using individualized schedules as a component of positive behavioral support for students with developmental disabilities. *Journal of Positive Behavior Interventions, 4,* 73–79.

Montague, M., & Renaldi, C. (2001). Classroom dynamics and children at-risk: A follow-up. *Learning Disability Quarterly, 24,* 75–83.

Moore, D.W., Anderson, A., & Kumar, K. (2005). Instructional adaptation in the management of escape-maintained behavior in a classroom. *Journal of Positive Behavior Interventions, 7,* 216–223.

Newcomer, L.L., & Lewis, T.J. (2004). Functional behavior assessment: An investigation of assessment reliability and effectiveness of function-based interventions. *Journal of Emotional and Behavioral Disorders, 12,* 168–181.

Pitcher, G.D., & Poland, S. (1992). *Crisis intervention in the schools.* New York: Guilford.

Presley, J.A., & Hughes, C. (2000). Peers as teachers of anger management to high school students with behavioral disorders. *Behavioral Disorders, 25,* 114–130.

Rasmussen, K., & O'Neill, R.E. (2006). The effects of fixed-time reinforcement schedules on problem behavior of children with emotional and behavioral disorders in a day-treatment classroom setting. *Journal of Applied Behavior Analysis, 39,* 453–457.

Reichle, J., & Johnston, S.S. (1993). Replacing challenging behavior: The role of communication intervention. *Topics in Language Disorders, 13,* 61–76.

Reimers, T., & Wacker, D. (1988). Parents' ratings of the acceptability of behavioral treatment recommendations made in an outpatient clinic: A preliminary analysis of the influence of treatment effectiveness. *Behavioral Disorders, 14,* 7–15.

Repp, A.C., & Horner, R.H. (Eds.). (1999). *Functional analysis of problem behavior: From effective assessment to effective support.* Belmont, CA: Wadsworth Publishing.

Rock, M.L., (2005). Use of strategic self-monitoring to enhance academic engagement, productivity, and accuracy of students with and without disabilities. *Journal of Positive Behavioral Interventions, 7,* 3–17.

Rock, M.L., & Thead, B.K. (2007). The effects of fading a strategic self-monitoring intervention on students' academic engagement, accuracy, and productivity. *Journal of Behavioral Education, 16,* 389–412.

Romaniuk, C., Miltenberger, R., Conyers, C., Jenner, N., Jurgens, M., & Ringenberg, C. (2002). The influence of activity choice on problem behaviors maintained by escape versus attention. *Journal of Applied Behavior Analysis, 35,* 349–362.

Sailor, W., Dunlap, G., Sugai, G., & Horner, R.H. (Eds.). (2009). *Handbook of positive behavior support.* New York: Springer.

Sainato, D.M., Strain, P.S., Lefebvre, D., & Rapp, N. (1987). Facilitating transition times with handicapped preschool children: A comparison between peer-mediated and antecedent prompt procedures. *Journal of Applied Behavior Analysis, 20,* 285–291.

Sasso, G.M., Reimers, T., Cooper, L., Wacker, D., Berg, W., Steege, M., et al. (1992). Use of descriptive and experimental analyses to identify the functional properties of aberrant behavior in school settings. *Journal of Applied Behavior Analysis, 25,* 809–821.

Schunk, D.H. (1987). Peer models and children's behavioral change. *Review of Educational Research, 57,* 149–174.

Shogren, K.A., Faggella-Luby, M.N., Bae, S.J. (2004). The effect of choice making as an intervention for problem behavior: A meta-analysis. *Journal of Positive Behavior Interventions, 6,* 228–237.

Shores, R.E., Gunter, P.L., & Jack, S.L. (1993). Classroom management strategies: Are they setting events for coercion? *Behavioral Disorders, 18,* 92–102.

Shores, R.E., Jack, S.L., Gunter, P.L., Ellis, D.N., DeBriere, T.J., & Wehby, J.H. (1993). Classroom interactions of children with behavior disorders. *Journal of Emotional and Behavioral Disorders, 1,* 27–39.

Shure, M.B. (1993). I can problem solve (ICPS): Interpersonal cognitive problem solving for your children. *Early Child Development and Care, 96*, 49–64.

Skinner, C.H., Skinner, A.L., & Sterling-Turner, H.E. (2002). Best practices in contingency management: Application of individual and group contingencies in educational settings. In A. Thomas & J. Grimes (Eds.), *Best practices in school psychology IV: Vol. 1, Vol. 2* (pp. 817–830). Washington, DC: National Association of School Psychologists.

Stahr, B., Cushing, D., Lane, K., & Fox, J. (2006). Efficacy of a function-based intervention in decreasing off-task behavior exhibited by a student with ADHD. *Journal of Positive Behavior Interventions, 8*, 201–211.

Stormont, M.A., Smith, S.C., & Lewis, T.J. (2007). Teacher implementation of pre-correction and praise statements in Head Start classrooms as a component of a program-wide system of positive behavior support. *Journal of Behavioral Education, 16*, 280–290.

Strain, P.S., Schwartz, I.S., & Bovey, E.H. (2008). Social competence interventions for young children with autism. In W.H. Brown, S.L. Odom, & S.R. McConnell (Eds.), *Social competence of young children: Risk, disability, and intervention* (pp. 253–272). Baltimore: Paul H. Brookes Publishing Co.

Strong, A.C., Wehby, J.H., Falk, K.B., & Lane, K.L. (2004). The impact of a structured reading curriculum and repeated reading on the performance of junior high students with emotional and behavioral disorders. *School Psychology Review, 33*, 561–581.

Sugai, G., & Chanter, C. (1989). The effects of training students with learning and behavior disorders to modify the behavior of their peers. *Education & Treatment of Children, 12*, 134–151.

Sutherland, K., & Snyder, A. (2007). Effects of reciprocal peer tutoring and self-graphing on reading fluency and classroom behavior of middle school students with emotional and behavioral disorders. *Journal of Emotional and Behavioral Disorders, 15*, 103–118.

Telecsan, B.L., Slaton, D.B., & Stevens, K.B. (1999). Peer tutoring: Teaching students with learning disabilities to deliver time delay instruction. *Journal of Behavioral Education, 9*, 133–154.

Theodore, L.A., Bray, M.A., & Kehle, T.J. (2004). A comparative study of group contingencies and randomized reinforcers to reduce disruptive classroom behavior. *School Psychology Quarterly, 19*, 253–271.

Tiger, J.H., Hanley, G.P., & Hernandez, E. (2006). An evaluation of the value of choice with preschool children. *Journal of Applied Behavior Analysis, 39*, 1–16.

Tralli, R., Colombo, B., Deshler, D.D., & Schumaker, J.B. (1996). The Strategies Intervention Model: A model for supported inclusion at the secondary level. *Remedial and Special Education, 17*, 204–216.

Tustin, R.D. (1995). The effects of advance notice of activity transitions on stereotypic behavior. *Journal of Applied Behavior Analysis, 28*, 91–92.

Umbreit, J., Ferro, J., Liaupsin, C., & Lane, K.L. (2007). *Functional behavioral assessment and function-based intervention: An effective, practical approach.* Englewood Cliffs, NJ: Merrill/Prentice Hall.

Vandercook, T., & York, J. (1990). A team approach to program development and support. In W.C. Stainback & S.B. Stainback (Eds.), *Support networks for inclusive schooling: Integrated and interdependent education* (pp. 95–122). Baltimore: Paul H. Brookes Publishing Co.

Vaughn, B.J., & Horner, R.H. (1997). Identifying instructional tasks that occasion problem behaviors and assessing the effects of student versus teacher choice among these tasks. *Journal of Applied Behavior Analysis, 30*, 299–312.

Villa, R.A., Thousand, J.S., Paolucci-Whitcomb, P., & Nevin, A.I. (1990). In search of a new paradigm for collaborative consultation. *Journal of Educational and Psychological Consultation, 1*, 279–292.

Webster-Stratton, C., Reid, J., & Hammond, M. (2001). Social skills and problem-solving training for children with early-onset conduct problems. Who benefits? *Journal of Child Psychology and Psychiatry, 42*, 943–952.

Werts, M.G., Caldwell, N.K., & Wolery, M. (1996). Peer modeling of response chains: Observational learning by students with disabilities. *Journal of Applied Behavior Analysis, 29*, 53–66.

Index

Throughout this index, the PTR acronym is used for Prevent-Teach-Reinforce and *f* indicates a figure on the page.